# HSK
# 中国汉语水平考试语法题解
## （初、中等）

## The Explanations of Keys to HSK Grammatical Section
## (Elementary & Intermediate)

英文注释本（with English translation）

编著　崔希亮　王小玲
翻译　韩振恒

北京语言大学出版社

中国国家汉办赠送
Donated by Hanban, China

(京) 新登字 157 号

图书在版编目（CIP）数据

HSK 中国汉语水平考试语法题解（初、中等）英文注释本/崔希亮，王小玲编著；韩振恒译．
- 北京：北京语言大学出版社，2004 重印
ISBN 7 - 5619 - 0998 - 5

Ⅰ．H…
Ⅱ．①崔…　②王…　③韩…
Ⅲ．汉语 - 语法 - 对外汉语教学 - 水平考试 - 解题
Ⅳ．H195 - 44

中国版本图书馆 CIP 数据核字（2001）第 072703 号

责任印制：乔学军
出版发行：北京语言大学出版社
社　　址：北京市海淀区学院路 15 号　邮政编码：100083
网　　址：http://www.blcup.com
印　　刷：北京北林印刷厂
经　　销：全国新华书店
版　　次：2001 年 12 月第 1 版　2004 年 2 月第 2 次印刷
开　　本：787 毫米×1092 毫米　1/16　印张：8.75
字　　数：149 千字　印数：5000 - 8000 册
书　　号：ISBN 7 - 5619 - 0998 - 5/H・01099
　　　　　2002 DW 0005
定　　价：20.50 元

出版部电话：010 - 82303590
发行部电话：010 - 82303651　82303591
　　传　真：010 - 82303081
E-mail：fxb@blcu.edu.cn

如有印装质量问题・本社出版部负责调换

# 目　录

编写说明

中国汉语水平考试语法结构(初、中等)模拟试卷 ……………………………（1）

中国汉语水平考试语法结构(初、中等)模拟试卷答案纸及标准答案 ………（4）

中国汉语水平考试语法结构(初、中等)模拟试卷题解 ………………………（5）

中国汉语水平考试语法结构(初、中等)甲级200题题解 ……………………（15）

中国汉语水平考试语法结构(初、中等)模拟练习 ……………………………（102）

中国汉语水平考试语法结构(初、中等)模拟练习答案 ………………………（132）

# 编写说明

• **编写目的**

中国汉语水平考试 HSK 是中国国家级标准化考试,它是专门为母语不是汉语的人而设立的水平测试。自 1990 年启动以来,已经在国内外设立了许多考点,参加考试的人数不断增加。随之而来的就是考生对参考资料的需求与日俱增。为了使学生在准备考试的时候能够比较好地掌握汉语的语法规律,我们编写了这本语法题解。读者对象为 HSK 考生和辅导教师。目前已经有汉语水平考试的模拟习题集出版,这对考生来说无疑是很有帮助的。习题集提供了模拟试卷和标准答案,但是对其中的语法问题没有提供一个简明易懂的解释,可以使学生在知其然的时候也能知其所以然。这本题解以国家汉语教学领导小组办公室汉语水平考试部制订的《汉语水平等级标准与语法等级大纲》(高等教育出版社 1996)和国家汉语水平考试委员会办公室编写的《汉语水平考试大纲》(初、中等)为基础,结合近年来现代汉语语法研究的最新成果,模拟 HSK 标准试卷,编制了适合初、中等汉语水平考生的试题,并对试题进行简单明了的解释说明,以期对辅导教师和考生有所帮助。

• **编写体例**

我们编写的这本《中国汉语水平考试语法题解》以《汉语水平等级标准与语法等级大纲》为依据,从甲级语法大纲到乙级语法大纲的语法项目都在我们题解的范围之内,其中第一分册是甲级题解,第二分册是乙级题解。在题解的每一部分,我们设计了一份与正式试卷形式相同的模拟考卷("语法结构"这一部分)。每张试卷 30 题,20 分钟。标准答案和题解附在试卷的后面。使用者可以先做模拟试题,然后对照参考答案进行自我评价,最后再根据语法题解找出自己出错的原因。在模拟考卷之后是我们依据《汉语水平等级标准与语法等级大纲》设计的类型题以及我们对这些问题语法项目的解释。

• **编者简介**

崔希亮,北京语言文化大学教授。1983 年毕业于北京大学中国语言文学系汉语专业,获得文学学士学位,1987 年在北京大学中国语言文学系现代汉语专业毕业,获文学硕士学位。1987 年到北京语言文化大学(原北京语言学院)语言文学系和留学生二系任教。现任北京语言文化大学校长助理,对外汉语研究中心副主任,世界汉语教学学会会员,中国语言学会会员,主要研究方向为现代汉语语法和汉语熟语,近年来发表了《汉语"连"字句的语用分析》、《"把"字句的若干句法语义问题》、《"在"字结构解析》等学术论文二十余篇,并出版了专著《汉语熟语与中国人文世界》。

王小玲,北京语言文化大学硕士研究生。1993年毕业于牡丹江师范学院中文系,1997年考入北京语言文化大学攻读硕士学位,2000年获得文学硕士学位。在读期间曾有文学作品发表。

参加编写的人员还有北京语言文化大学语言文学系教师姚洪昌,北京语言文化大学的研究生周荣和杜新天。甲级题解的试题部分由崔希亮、王小玲、姚洪昌共同编写,其中王小玲承担了大部分试题的编写工作。题解部分由崔希亮编写,北京语言文化大学研究生周荣、杜新天也参加了题解的初期编写工作。模拟试题由王小玲编写。最后由崔希亮统稿。感谢我的学生王小玲以及她的先生赵宾,他们对这本小册子的编写投入了极大的热情。

我还要特别感谢日本御茶之水女子大学的博士研究生、北京语言文化大学高级进修生森中野枝女士,她承担了《题解》日本语的翻译工作,同时也对文稿中的一些问题提出了中肯的意见;我还要感谢韩振恒先生承担了《题解》英文翻译工作;我也要感谢北京语言文化大学高级进修生卢智暎女士,她承担了《题解》韩国语的翻译工作。语法题解翻译起来困难很大,因此我对他们的工作表示由衷的敬佩。最后我要感谢北京语言文化大学出版社的王建勤社长和沈庶英女士,没有王建勤的建议我不会做这项工作;沈庶英则为文稿的最后成型花费了大量心血,她的耐心和对我工作进度的宽容使我能够比较从容地完成细部刻画,使题解部分不至于太过粗糙。其中可能会有不少疏漏和谬误之处,这全都由我个人负责。

但愿这本小册子能够对学习汉语的留学生和汉语教师有所帮助。

崔希亮
2001年3月12日

# 中国汉语水平考试语法结构
## （初、中等）
## 模拟试卷

### 二、语法结构
（30题，20分钟）

#### 第一部分

说明：51~60题，在每一个句子下面都有一个指定词语，句中A、B、C、D是供选择的四个不同位置，请判断这一词语放在句子中哪个位置上恰当。

例如：

　　55.我们A一起B去上海C旅游D过。

　　　　没有

"没有"只有放在A的位置上，使全句变为"我们没有一起去上海旅游过"，才合乎语法。所以第55题惟一恰当的答案是A，你应在答卷上找到号码55，在字母A上画一横道，横道一定要画得粗一些，重一些。

55.[★]　　[B]　　[C]　　[D]

51.A你B告诉我教室C在D什么地方吗？

　　　　能

52.我A昨天B是跟他C去的图书馆D。

　　　　一起

53.我A一个同事的女儿，B是C您D影迷。

　　　　也

54.校长A两位B女士C让D进屋。

　　　　把

55.一个A大明星B住在C这么个D小破屋子里。

　　　　就

56.我A觉得女同志B要长就应该C长出自己的特点D。

　　　　来

57.这A工作B是个很容易C让人产生误会的D工作。

　　　　本来

58. A 要求 B 得到精神满足 C 不是少数人的 D 特权。

59. 一个国家是否 A 现代，除了 B 看它的工农业发展水平，C 要 D 看它的科技水平。

60. 我 A 从小就有个理想，一直 B 没实现，C 而且恐怕 D 没指望实现了。

已
还
越来越

## 第二部分

说明：61~80题，每个句子中有一个或两个空儿，请在A、B、C、D四个答案中选择惟一恰当的填上(在答卷上的字母上画一横道)。

例如：

67. 我昨天买了一_____钢笔。

A. 件　　B. 块　　C. 枝　　D. 条

我们只能说"我昨天买了一枝钢笔"，所以第67题惟一恰当的答案是C，你应在答卷上找到号码67，在字母C上画一横道，横道一定要画得粗一些，重一些。

67. [A]　　[B]　　[C]　　[D]

61. 他给女友买了一_____手表。
   A. 块
   B. 条
   C. 棵
   D. 件

62. 我找到了一家既便宜_____干净的旅馆。
   A. 再
   B. 又
   C. 越
   D. 有

63. 这个房间_____布置成会客厅。
   A. 使
   B. 把
   C. 让
   D. 被

64. 同学们是骑自行车去_____。
   A. 的
   B. 了
   C. 着
   D. 呢

65. 突然，一辆大卡车_____极快的速度冲了过来。
   A. 以
   B. 按
   C. 凭
   D. 由

66. 他_____工作努力，今年得到了国家奖学金。
   A. 关于
   B. 对于
   C. 由于
   D. 在于

67. 这些餐馆的出现_____吃饭不再困难。
   A. 令
   B. 使
   C. 叫
   D. 让

68. 我们明天还是先打个电话_____去。
   A. 再
   B. 还
   C. 又
   D. 也

69. 他们先_____鸟笼子挂好,找地方坐下。
   A. 把          B. 使
   C. 对          D. 让

70. 这场战争要是真打_____,人类的末日就要到了。
   A. 上来        B. 起来
   C. 出来        D. 进来

71. 北京的冬天很冷,_____人们要穿厚衣服。
   A. 所以        B. 因为
   C. 不过        D. 如果

72. 无论大人孩子都要买票,_____是刚出生的婴儿也要买票。
   A. 尽管        B. 即使
   C. 如果        D. 只要

73. 这么简单的道理连三岁的孩子都懂,_____你真的不懂?
   A. 难道        B. 何况
   C. 既然        D. 但是

74. _____叫别人来管理这个企业,不如我们自己管理。
   A. 与其        B. 即使
   C. 于是        D. 不论

75. 他一个人在草地上_____。
   A. 走来走去
   B. 走走来去
   C. 走来走走
   D. 走来去去

76. 那棵树已经有100多年了,_____。
   A. 仍然现在长得很茂盛。
   B. 现在仍然长得很茂盛。
   C. 长得仍然现在很茂盛。
   D. 仍然长得现在很茂盛。

77. 代表团于9月26号_____。
   A. 乘飞机回到北京从纽约。
   B. 从纽约回到北京乘飞机。
   C. 从纽约乘飞机回到北京。
   D. 从乘飞机纽约回到北京。

78. 汉字很不容易写,_____。
   A. 苦工夫不下学不好。
   B. 不下苦工夫不学好。
   C. 不下苦工夫不好学。
   D. 不下苦工夫学不好。

79. 去年买的那件雨衣已经破了,_____。
   A. 一定今年得买一件结实点。
   B. 一定得买一件结实点的今年。
   C. 今年一定得买一件结实点的。
   D. 今年得买一定一件结实点的。

80. 推土机正在_____。
   A. 日夜不停地在为新的宿舍楼平整地基。
   B. 日夜不停地平整地基在为新的宿舍楼。
   C. 在为新的宿舍楼平整地基日夜不停地。
   D. 在为新的宿舍楼日夜不停地平整地基。

# 答案纸及标准答案

| # | Answer | # | Answer |
|---|---|---|---|
| 51 | | 51 | B |
| 52 | | 52 | C |
| 53 | | 53 | B |
| 54 | | 54 | A |
| 55 | | 55 | B |
| 56 | | 56 | D |
| 57 | | 57 | |
| 58 | | 58 | C |
| 59 | | 59 | C |
| 60 | | 60 | D |
| 61 | | 61 | A |
| 62 | | 62 | A |
| 63 | | 63 | D |
| 64 | | 64 | A |
| 65 | | 65 | |
| 66 | | 66 | C |
| 67 | | 67 | B |
| 68 | | 68 | A |
| 69 | | 69 | A |
| 70 | | 70 | B |
| 71 | | 71 | A |
| 72 | | 72 | B |
| 73 | | 73 | A |
| 74 | | 74 | A |
| 75 | | 75 | A |
| 76 | | 76 | B |
| 77 | | 77 | C |
| 78 | | 78 | D |
| 79 | | 79 | C |
| 80 | | 80 | A |

## 模拟试卷题解

51. 正确答案只能是 B,因为能愿动词必须放在主要动词前。这样就排除了 A 和 D 这两个位置。这个句子是一个比较复杂的双宾语疑问句,主要结构为"你能告诉我[……]吗?"其中[……]部分又是一个主谓结构。所以句子中有两个动词:"告诉"和"在"。问题的关键在于判断哪一个是主要动词。

52. 正确答案是 C,因为"一起"是一个副词,副词在句子结构里应该放在动词前面做状语。这个句子有两个动词:"是"和"去"。根据副词"一起"的意义我们知道它所修饰限制的行为动作一定是一个动态的、可以描述的动作,而"是"是一个抽象程度比较高的动词,不适合于接受"一起"的修饰限制。A 位于时间名词前,D 位于句末,都可以排除在外。

53. 正确答案只能是 B,因为"也"是副词,而副词只能出现在动词前,这个句子只有一个动词"是",因此很容易判断。

54. 这个句子正确答案是 A。从这个句子的结构来看,有两个名词性的主目(argument),一个谓项(predicate),而且是一个结果性很强的谓项,因此句子可能是"把"字句(causative)或者"被动句"(passive voice)。可选择的答案是"把",由此可以判断是"把"字句。"把"字结构的典型形式为:

主目$_1$(causer) + 把 + 主目$_2$(causee) + VC

在这个句子里,"校长"是主目$_1$,两位女士是主目$_2$,因此"把"字只能放在两者之间。因此 C 和 D 两个位置可以排除了。"两位"和"女士"是数量名结构,不能插入介词。所以 B 也被排除了。

55. 正确答案是 B。"就"是副词,通常用在动词前做状语。这个句子只有一个动词"住",因此答案比较可能是"住"前面的 B。但是我们还应该知道:"就"也可以用在"指示代词 + 名词"前,如"就这么个小东西要我 200 块钱","就这么个小破屋子还等了 10 年"。所以 C 也可能是正确答案。为什么选择 B 不选择 C 呢?因为在这个句子里"指示代词 + 名词"是嵌套在方位结构"在……里"的,"就"不能出现在"在"后。所以只有 B 是正确答案。

56. 正确答案是 D。这个句子有"动词 + 出"这个结构,一般说来,"出"后边要有"来"做它的后续成分。那么 D 在"出"字之后。

57. 正确答案是 B。"本来"有两种词性:形容词和副词。形容词的"本来"意思是"原有的",可以修饰名词,但是他能修饰的名词很有限,如"本来面目",很少见到与其他名词搭配。副词的"本来"用在动词前,意思是"原先的,先前的,按道理说应该这样的"。这个句子有三个动词:"是"、"让"和"产生",但是只有 B 和 C 两个位置可供选择。C 前边有其他的修饰成分,不容易再插入一个副词,因此"本来"最可能出现的位置是 B。再参考"本来"的意思就可以肯定 B 是惟一正确的位置。

58．正确答案是 C。"已"是副词,跟"未"相对,应该出现在动词或动词性成分前,而这个动词或动词性成分必须是包含完句成分的,也就是说它后边的成分必须包含一个完整的逻辑谓项。这个句子有三个动词"要求"、"得到"和"是"。只有 C 后边的成分包含一个完整的逻辑谓项。

59．正确答案是 C。"除了……还"是常用的关联形式,连接两个句法地位平等的结构。这个句子"看它的工农业发展水平"和"要看它的科技水平"是两个平等的结构,所以 C 是最恰当的位置。有时候这个关联形式连接的两个成分看上去好像不是性质相同、语法地位平等的句法成分,那是因为可能有省略了的成分,例如"除了张三,还有李四也去了","张三"后面省略了"去了"。

60．正确答案是 D。"越来越"是副词,用在谓词(形容词和动词)性成分前,意思是随着某个条件的变化,谓词性成分所指涉的内容程度递进加深。如"越来越好"、"越来越胖"、"越来越不听话"、"越来越没信心"等。这个句子"而且"后边的成分可以表示递进,所以 D 是"越来越"最恰当的位置。

61．正确答案是 A。"手表"的量词是"块"。

62．正确答案是 B。"既……又"是固定搭配。

63．正确答案是 D。这个句子的主语是个受事,又不是指使者(causer),因此"使"、"把"可以排除在正确答案之外。剩下的"让"和"被"是可能的选择。但是"让"出现在被动句的时候必须有施事同时出现,这个句子没有施事,所以只能是"被"。

64．正确答案是 A。"是……的"是固定搭配。

65．正确答案是 A。介词"以"、"按"、"凭"和"由"都可以和名词"速度"构成介词结构。"以+名词"引出方式或标准,"按+名词"引出凭借物或者规则,"凭+名词"引出依据或者凭借理由,"由+名词"引出路径或者凭借物,或者施动者。这个句子"速度"是方式,因此选 A。

66．正确答案是 C。"关于"、"对于"和"在于"都是介词,它们与后边的名词构成介词结构做状语。"由于"是连词,连接两个谓词性成分。在这个句子中,"工作努力"和"得到了国家奖学金"是两个谓词性成分。

67．正确答案是 B。"令"、"使"、"叫"、"让"都有使令义,但是它们的用法不同。"令"、"叫"、"让"后边必须是一个兼语结构,而"使"后边可以是兼语结构,也可以是主谓结构。这个句子中的"吃饭不再困难"是主谓结构而不是兼语结构。另外,"使"的致使意义更强,因此它要求后边的成分带有结果性。

68．正确答案是 A。副词"再"、"还"、"又"、"也"在意义上都可以表示动作

(或状态)的继续或者重复,但是在这个句子里,并不是要表达动作(或状态)的继续或重复,而是要表达一个事件和前一个事件紧接着发生,那就只有"再"与"先"一起才能胜任。

69. 正确答案是 A。"把"和"对"是介词,"使"和"让"是动词。这里应该出现的是介词,所以"使"和"让"被排除了。"鸟笼子挂好"是个复杂形式,结果意义明显,符合"把"字出现的条件;"挂"是动态动词,处置意义很鲜明,因此需要句子的主语具有[+施事]这样的语义特征,而主语"他们"恰好具有这样的语义特征。这个句子符合"把"字结构成立的所有条件,按照答案只有一个的原则,我们选择"把"。

70. 正确答案是 B。"上来"、"起来"、"出来"、"进来"都是复合趋向动词,它们本身都有实在意思。它们也都可以用在动词后充当补语,充当补语时有时是实在意思(本义),有时是虚指义。"上来"、"起来"多用于虚指,"出来"、"进来"多用本义。判断它们是本义还是虚指义主要要看动词的语义类型,说得再具体些是要看动词的抽象程度。抽象程度越深,虚指义的可能性也就越大。"打(战争)"抽象程度比较深,因此可以判断它们在这个句子里是虚指义。同样是用在动词后边,它们的意思却不一样。但是每一个都有许多义项。我们只考虑与"打"结合以后的那个义项。"上来"用在动词后表示说、唱、背诵等成功,"起来"表示动作或者时间开始并持续。根据句子的意思,应该选择"起来"。

71. 正确答案是 A。"所以"、"因为"、"不过"、"如果"都是关联词,"所以"连接因果关系的结果部分,"因为"连接因果关系的原因部分,"不过"连接转折关系的两个小句,"如果"连接假设关系的两个小句。这个句子前后两个小句的关系显然是因果关系,所以 A 为正确答案。

72. 正确答案是 B。"尽管"、"即使"、"如果"、"只要"都是关联词语。"尽管"表示姑且先承认某种事实,下文紧接着提出相反的意见或论据,往往有"但是""然而"等表示转折的关联词语;"即使"表示假设的让步,它所连接的命题常常是一个比较极端的例子;"如果"单纯表示假设;"只要"表示最小条件。根据句义,"刚出生的婴儿也要买票"是一个假设的极端的例子,所以应选择"即使"。

73. 正确答案是 A。"难道"是一个加强反问语气的副词。"何况"、"既然"、"但是"都不表示反问。这里是一个反问句,只能选择"难道"。

74. 正确答案是 A。"与其……不如"是一个固定搭配,表示取舍。

75. 正确答案是 A。动词与"来"、"去"结合只有三种形式:(1) V 来/V 去;(2) 来 V/去 V;(3) V 来 V 去。所以只有"走来走去"是对的。

76. 正确答案是 B。"现在仍然长得很茂盛"结构顺序很正确,意义很通顺。它的结构层次和结构关系是这样的:

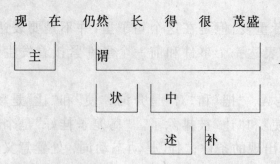

另外三个小句不能作这样的分析。因为它们的语序都有问题。

77. 正确答案是C。整个句子的结构层次和结构关系是这样的：

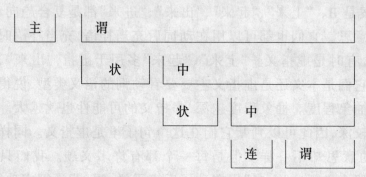

在现代汉语中，状语永远在谓词性成分的前面。介词结构做状语也必须放在谓词性成分的前面。这样A就是错的。介词结构中的介词与名词联系很紧密，因此D也是错的。连谓结构的两个谓词性成分在意义上有联系，如果表达先后进行的两件事，那么应该按事物发生的先后顺序排列，因此B也是错的。

78. 正确答案是D。汉语是SVO型语言，答案A的动词在宾语后不符合汉语SVO的结构顺序。汉语表示可能的补语有"V得C"和"V不C"两种形式，没有"不VC"，所以答案B也是错的。答案C"不下苦功夫不好学"语法上是可以接受的，但是意义上有毛病，一是与上一句缺乏逻辑上的联系，二是它本身也不合常理，因为好学不好学与下苦工夫没有必然联系。用归余法我们知道只有D是正确答案。

79. 正确答案是C。答案A中的副词"一定"应该放在动词"得"之前，而不是放在整个句子的主语之前，所以答案A是错的。答案B把主语"今年"放在了句尾，所以也是错的。答案D把副词"一定"放在了动词后边，所以也是错的。这样，只有答案C是对的。

80. 正确答案是A。在现代汉语中，表示目的的成分和表示手段的成分同时出现时，目的在先，手段放在后边，答案B错在把目的"在为新的宿舍楼"放在了手段"平整地基"之后。答案C和答案D错在两个"在"对接在一起，违反了言语表达中简约的原则和清晰的原则。答案C还把状语放在了动词之后，这在汉语中也是违反常规的。

# Keys to the Simulated Test

51. The correct answer can only be B for the reason that the modal verbs must be put before the main verbs. In this way, the two positions indicated by answers A and D can be ruled out. This is a rather complicated double-object interrogative sentence, whose main structure is "你能告诉我［……］吗?", in which the ［……］ part is a subject-predicate structure. Therefore, there are two verbs in the sentence, "告诉" and "在". The key to the question is to judge which is the main verb.

52. The correct answer is C, for the reason that "一起" is an adverb, which should be put before a verb to function as an adverbial in a sentence. In this sentence, there are two verbs: "是" and "去". From the meaning of the adverb "一起", we know that the action it modifies must be a dynamic and describable action while "是" is a verb that is too abstract to be modified by "一起". For the reason that answer A lies before the time noun and answer D lies at the end of the sentence, they can all be ruled out.

53. The correct answer can only be B for the reason that "也" is an adverb, which can appear only before a verb. In this sentence, there is only one verb which is "是", and therefore it is very easy to judge.

54. The correct answer to this sentence is A. From the point of view of the structure of the sentence, there are two nominal elements ("校长"、"两位女士") and one predicate element ("让进屋"). The element that is to be embedded is the character "把", and therefore we can conclude that it is a "把" sentence. The typical structure of "把" sentence is as follows:

$$NP_1(causer) + 把 + NP_2(causee) + VC$$

In this sentence, "校长" is $NP_1$ and "两位女士" is $NP_2$. Therefore, the character "把" can only be put between the two nominal elements. So both of the positions indicated by answers C and D can be ruled out. "两位" and "女士" is a measure-word-noun structure, in which no preposition is to be inserted. So answer B can be ruled out.

55. The correct answer is B. "就" is an adverb, which usually appears before a verb to function as an adverbial. In this sentence, there is only one verb "住". Therefore, the possible answer might be B before "住". We should also know that, however, "就" can also be used before the structure of "demonstrative pronoun + noun", for example: "就这么个小东西要我 200 块钱" and "就这么个小破屋子还等了 10 年". So C might also be the correct answer. The reason that B is chosen instead of C is that in this sentence, "demonstrative pronoun + noun" is used in the structure indicating the direction and position, "在……里", and "就" cannot appear after "在". So only B is the correct answer.

56. The correct answer is D. In this sentence, there is the structure of "verb + 出". Generally speaking, there should be "来" to be used after "出" to function as its

following element. And answer D just appears after "出".

57. The correct answer is B. "本来" can function as two kinds of part of speech: adjective and adverb. The adjective "本来" has the meaning of "原有的(original)", and it can be used to modify nouns. The nouns it can modify, however, are limited, for example: "本来面貌". It is rarely used together with other nouns. The adverb "本来" is used before verbs, meaning "原先的、先前的、按道理说应该这样的 (originally, previously, it should be so according to the common sense)". In this sentence, there are three verbs: "是", "让" and "产生", among which, only the two positions of B and C could be selected. Before C there are already other modifying elements and it is very hard to insert another adverb between them. Therefore, the most possible position where "本来" could appear is B. And given the meaning of "本来", it can be assured that B is the only correct position.

58. The correct answer is C. "已" is an adverb, which is opposite to "未" in the meaning. It should appear before verbs or verbal elements which should include in it a predicative object, that is to say, the element after it must include a complete sub-clause object. In this sentence, there are three verbs: "要求", "得到" and "是", among which, only the element after C has a complete logic predicate element in it.

59. The correct answer is C. "除了……还" is a commonly-used structure, which connects two structures with equal syntactic status. In this sentence, "看它的工农业发展水平" and "要看它的科技水平" are two equal structures, so C is the most suitable position for the embedded character "还".

60. The correct answer is D. "越来越" is an adverb used before predicative elements (adjective and verb) to mean that along with the changes of a certain condition, the extent of the thing referred to by the predicative element is growing and deepening, for example: "越来越好", "越来越胖", "越来越不听话" and "越来越没信心", etc. In this sentence, the element after "而且" can indicate the increase by degrees. So D is the most suitable position of "越来越".

61. The correct answer is A. The measure word of "手表" is "块".

62. The correct answer is B. "既……又" is a fixed collocation.

63. The correct answer is D. The subject of the sentence is the receiver of the action, not the causer. Therefore, "使" and "把" can be ruled out from the correct answer. The remaining "让" and "被" are possible choices. But when "让" appears in a passive voice sentence, the agent must appear simultaneously. In this sentence, there is no agent, and so the only choice is "被".

64. The correct answer is A. "是……的" is a fixed collocation.

65. The correct answer is A. The prepositions "以", "按", "凭" and "由" can all form prepositional structures with "速度". The structure of "以 + nouns" indicates the way or the standard of doing something, "按 + nouns" indicates the objects to be depended or rules to be followed, "凭 + nouns" introduces the basis or the reason to be

relied, and "由 + nouns" introduces the agents or the objects to be depended. In this sentence, "速度" is the way or standard of driving, and therefore answer A should be chosen as the correct one.

66. The correct answer is C. "关于", "对于" and "在于" are all prepositions. They can be used to form prepositional structures with the noun following them to function as adverbials. "由于" is a conjunction connecting two predicative elements. In this sentence, "工作努力" and "得到了国家奖学金" are two predicative elements.

67. The correct answer is B. "令", "使", "叫" and "让" all have an imperative meaning, but they have different usages. There must be a concurrent element after "令", "叫" and "让", while there can be a concurrent element or a subject-predicate structure after "使". In this sentence, "吃饭不再困难" is a subject-predicate structure instead of a concurrent element structure. Furthermore, "使" has a stronger sense of causing, and so it demands that the element following it be result oriented.

68. The correct answer is A. The adverbs "再", "还", "又" and "也" can all be used to indicate the lasting or repeating of an action (or state). But in this sentence, what is to be expressed is not the lasting or repeating of an action, but that two events happened closely one after the other. In this case, only the combination of "再" with "也" can express this meaning.

69. The correct answer is A. "把" and "对" are prepositions, while "使" and "让" are verbs. What should appear here should be a preposition. So "使" and "让" are ruled out. "鸟笼子挂好了" is a complicated phrase indicating a strong sense of result and meets the conditions for "把" sentence to appear. "挂" is a dynamic verb with a strong sense of dealing with something. So it requires that the subject of the sentence has the semantic characteristics of [ + agent]. And the subject "他们" just has such a semantic characteristics. This sentence meets all the conditions for the "把" structure to stand. Given that there should be one answer, we choose "把".

70. The correct answer is B. "上来", "起来", "出来" and "进来" are all compound verbs indicating directions with substantial meanings by themselves. They can all be used after verbs to function as complements. When it functions as a complement, it can either have substantial meanings or just indicate a trend without substantial meanings. "上来" and "起来" are more often used for empty references, and "出来" and "进来" are more often used with their original meanings. The way to judge whether they are used for their original meanings or for empty reference meanings is to see what semantic type a verb belongs to. To be more specific, it depends on the extent of abstractness of the verb. The more abstract the verb is, the more possible that it is used for its empty reference. "打(战争)" is more abstract, and so it can be concluded that they are used in the sentence for empty reference. Although they can all be used after a verb, they could have different meanings. Each one of them has many semantic items and we now give our consideration only to that semantic item that combines with "打". "上来", used after a

verb, means the completion of such actions as speaking, singing, and reciting, etc. "起来" indicates the starting and continuing of an action or the time. According to the meaning of the sentence, "起来" should be chosen.

71. The correct answer is A. "所以", "因为", "不过", and "如果" are all relational words. What is introduced by "所以" is the result, and what is introduced by "因为" is the cause of the cause-result relations. "不过" connects two clauses that indicate a turning relationship, and "如果" connects two clauses indicating hypothesis. Here in this sentence, the relationship between the two clauses is obviously that of cause-result. So A is the correct answer.

72. The correct answer is B. "尽管", "即使", "如果", and "只要" are all relational words. "尽管" first takes something as a fact for the moment, and then immediately raises a contrary opinion or evidence. In this situation, there are usually such turning relational words as "但是" and "然而". "即使" indicates the concession to the assumed condition, and the proposition connected by it is usually an extreme example. "如果" solely indicates hypothesis. "只要" indicates the minimum condition. According to the meaning of the sentence, "刚出生的婴儿也要买票" is an assumed extreme example, and so "即使" should be chosen as the correct one.

73. The correct answer is A. "难道" is an adverb used to strengthen the tone of rhetoric question. None of "何况", "既然" and "但是" could be used to indicate the rhetoric tone. This is a rhetoric question, and so only "难道" can be chosen.

74. The correct answer is A. "与其……不如" is a fixed collocation indicating the meaning of rather than or better than.

75. The correct answer is A. When a verb is combined with "来" and "去", there could only be one of the following three situations: (1) V 来/V 去, (2) 来 V/去 V, (3) V 来 V 去. In this way, only "走来走去" is correct.

76. The correct answer is B. The order of the structure "现在仍然长得很茂盛" is correct and it is natural and fluent in meaning. Its structural levels and relations are as follows:

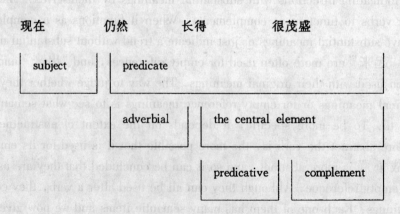

The other three clauses cannot be analyzed in this way because all of them have problems in the syntactic order.

77. The correct answer is C. The structural levels and structural relationships are as follows:

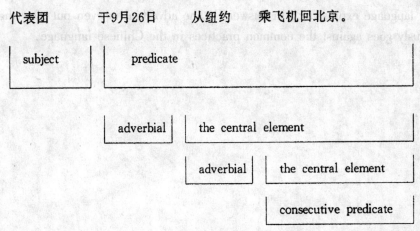

In modern Chinese, the adverbial is always put before the predicative element. Even if the adverbial is a prepositional structure, it must be put before the predicative element. Therefore answer A is wrong. In a prepositional structure, the preposition is usually put closely with the noun. So answer D is also wrong. The two predicative elements in a consecutive predicative structure are related to each other in the meanings. If they are two things that happen one after the other, they should be arranged according to the time order of their happening. In this way, answer B is also wrong.

78. The correct answer is D. The basic pattern of the Chinese language is SVO. In answer A, the verb has been put behind the object, which does not fit into the structural order of SVO. In the Chinese language, there are two forms of complement indicating possibility: "V 得 C" and "V 不 C", and there is no such form as "不 VC". So answer B is also wrong. In answer C, "不下苦功夫不好学" is acceptable in terms of grammar, but there are problems in meaning. On the one hand, it lacks a logical connection with the prior sentence; and on the other hand, it does not go along well with the common sense, because whether it is easy to learn or not is not necessarily decided by the fact that one works hard or not. In this way, only answer D is correct.

79. The correct answer is C. The adverb "一定" in answer A should be put before the verb "得", not at the front of the subject of the whole sentence. So answer A is wrong. In answer B, the subject "今年" is put at the end of the sentence, and thus it is also wrong. In answer D, the adverb "一定" is put behind the verb and thus it is wrong too. So only answer C is correct.

80. The correct answer is A. In modern Chinese, when the element indicating purpose and the element indicating method appear in a sentence simultaneously, the element

indicating purpose always comes first, and the element indicating the method the second. In answer B, the element indicating the purpose "在为新的宿舍楼" is put after the element indicating the method "平整地基" by mistake. What is wrong in answers C and D is that the two "在" are jointed together, thus violating the principle of being concise and clear in language expressing. In answer C, the adverbial is even put after the verb, and it obviously goes against the common practices in the Chinese language.

# 中国汉语水平考试语法结构
# （初、中等）甲级 200 题题解

## 选择填空题

### 时间词

1. 我将于_____抵达北京，请接站。
   A. 3 月 6 日,1999 年           B. 6 日 3 月,1999 年
   C. 1999 年 3 月 6 日           D. 1999 年 6 日 3 月

   题解：正确答案是 C。中国人的思维习惯一般是从大到小，比如指时间时，逻辑顺序为年、月、日、时、分、秒；指地点时，逻辑顺序为国、省、县、乡等，所以此题应选 D。

2. _____我在图书馆门口等你。
   A. 星期四下午两点半           B. 下午两点半星期四
   C. 两点半下午星期四           D. 两点半下午星期四

   题解：正确答案是 A。理由同上。

3. _____他还没有毕业呢。
   A. 在去年今天                 B. 在去年这天
   C. 今天的去年                 D. 去年的今天

   题解：正确答案是 D。因为中国人的思维习惯一般是从大到小，时间顺序上常为年、月、日、时、分、秒，所以此题首先排除 C；此题中的"去年"修饰"今天"，二者之间有领属关系，所以不能省略"的"，否则会引起逻辑上的矛盾。"在……今天"、"在……这天"都是介词结构，不能用做主语，所以 A、B 也不对。

### 名词重叠

4. 在新年的钟声敲响的时候，我深深地祝愿_____！
   A. 每家幸福,每人快乐           B. 家家幸福,人人快乐
   C. 每个家幸福,每个人快乐       D. 每一家幸福,每一人快乐

   题解：正确答案是 B。祝福的惯用语。汉语中有些可以作为临时量词用的名词重叠后具有周遍意义，即表示"所有的……都"，重叠后只能做主语。"每"指代的是某一个范围内全体成员中的任意一个成员，而不是指代全体成员，强调个体，不强调全体。

5. ＿＿＿＿＿＿终于盼到了这一天。

    A．年年盼，月月盼，天天盼    B．一年盼，一月盼，一天盼
    C．每个年盼，每个月盼，每个天盼  D．每年年盼，每月月盼，每天天盼

**题解**：正确答案是 A。理由同上。表示时间的名词重叠以后表示某一范围内的全体，表示"毫无例外"。"一"和"每"都指代个体，不能代表全体。

## 代词

6. 他这个人＿＿＿＿＿＿这么不讲道理？

    A．谁            B．什么
    C．怎么          D．怎么样

**题解**：正确答案是 C。这里缺的是一个状语，而"谁"、"什么"是体词性的，在句中的位置和名词完全一样，不能做状语，所以 A、B 可以排除。另外，这是个反问句，又是询问原因的，而 D"怎么样"询问的是方式，所以只能选 C。

7. 这个电影院有＿＿＿＿＿＿座位？

    A．几            B．几个
    C．多            D．多少

**题解**：正确答案是 D。这里缺少的是一个问数目的疑问代词，而"多"是形容词，所以 C 排除。"几"、"几个"用来替代一至十之间的待定数字，所以可以排除 A、B，而"多少"能替代任一待定数字，大小均可。另外，"几"与名词连用时，中间通常要插入适当的量词，因此不能选 A；而"多少"与名词连用时，其间的量词可有可无，所以选 D 是正确的。

8. 这位先生是你＿＿＿＿＿＿人？

    A．谁            B．什么
    C．哪            D．怎么

**题解**：正确答案是 B。这里缺少定语。"谁"做定语时，后面一般用结构助词"的"，表示领属关系。所以 A 可排除。"什么"做定语表修饰关系时，后边一般不用"的"。"哪"后往往带量词或数量词，所以 C 可排除。"怎么"放在"人"前时，也需加"个"，且是用于询问性质和状态的，D 也被排除了。这里"什么人"表示的是"这位先生"和"你"的关系。

9. 你看的是＿＿＿＿＿＿书？

    A．什么          B．谁
    C．怎么样         D．哪

**题解**：正确答案是 A。"谁"、"怎么样"、"哪"做定语修饰名词时必须加结构助词"的"。因此 B、C、D 都被排除了。

10. 您在_____个中学教书?
    A. 哪                           B. 谁
    C. 什么                         D. 怎么样

**题解**:正确答案是 A。第一,这里只有"哪"可放于量词或数量词前。第二,"谁"是问人的,"什么"是问事物的,"怎么"是问方式的。

11. 对待这种人你又能_____?
    A. 怎么                         B. 什么
    C. 哪里                         D. 怎么样

**题解**:正确答案是 D。这里需要询问方式、状况的疑问代词,"什么"是问事物的,"哪里"是问地点的,所以可排除 B、C。做谓语时,"怎么"后一般要用"了"或其他动词,排除 A。"怎么样"后不一定用"了",也不一定要用其他动词,所以 D 是正确的。

12. 他的生活_____有了些改善。
    A. 谁                           B. 多少
    C. 几                           D. 怎么样

**题解**:正确答案是 B。这是一个陈述句,缺少的是一个状语。而"谁"、"几"不能做状语,"怎么样"虽能做状语,但是个疑问代词,用于疑问句中。因此只能选 B。需要说明的是,"多少"是疑问代词,但是在这个句子里它兼有副词的功能,它做副词不表示疑问,而是表示数量。

13. 他四处漂泊几十年,_____苦没吃过?
    A. 什么                         B. 怎么
    C. 多么                         D. 这么

**题解**:正确答案是 A。这里缺少一个表泛指的疑问代词做定语,因为"苦"在这里是名词,意义为"苦难,艰苦的经历",属于事物范畴。只有 A 符合条件。"怎么"是指代方式的,"多么"、"这么"是指代程度的,修饰谓词。

14. 我好像在_____地方见过你。
    A. 哪里                         B. 几
    C. 怎么                         D. 什么

**题解**:正确答案是 D。"地方"是名词,属于事物范畴,应该用指代事物的代词"什么"来修饰,"几"是指代数量的,"怎么"是指代方式的,都不合适。此外,"哪里"是指代地点、方所的,"地方"从意思上说也是指代地点、方所的,"哪里"和"地方"语义重叠,所以也不能用"哪里"修饰"地方"。

15. 我还有_____百块钱,够买书了。
    A. 几多                         B. 几个
    C. 几                           D. 多

**题解**：正确答案是 C。"几"的用法有两个：第一个是疑问代词，询问从一到十的数量，例如"几个"、"几年"。第二是不定数词，表示不定的数量（从一到十）。它出现的位置是：可以在数量表达的"系数词 + 位数词"这个结构中，出现在系数词的位置上，代替系数词，和"十、百、千、万、亿"等位数词一起，表示"二十"以上概数，如："几十本书"、"几十人"、"几百年"等。"几"还可以出现在位数词的位置上，表示从一到九的数量，例如"十几"、"二十几"。"几多"是方言词，表示"多少"，后边不能有位数词，因此 A 不对；"几个"在和位数词搭配时只限于"亿"，如"几个亿"，但不能说"几个百"、"几个千"；"多"指数量大，但是并不是指数代词，而是形容词。

16. 这间教室没有那间教室_____大。

    A．这么                      B．那么

    C．这里                      D．那里

**题解**：正确答案是 B。这里需要一个表程度的指示代词，而 C、D 是称代处所的，所以应排除。"那间教室"又是表远指的，所以用 B"那么"。我们说"这间教室没有那间教室那么大"，也可以说"那间教室没有这间教室这么小"。

17. 请把_____三张桌子抬到 205 房间。

    A．这些                      B．这儿

    C．这                        D．哪

**题解**：正确答案是 C。"这些"的"些"是不定量词，表示约数或部分，所以后边不可再加确定的数词，也不能再有量词，故 A 可排除。"这儿"指代处所，排除 B。"哪"是疑问代词，此句却是祈使句，不是疑问句，也应排除 D。"这"与名词或"数量词 + 名词"连用时，可以起对人、对事物确指的作用。

18. 我的作业本在_____。

    A．老师                      B．老师里

    C．老师那儿              D．那老师

**题解**：正确答案是 C。汉语里有些动词如："来、去、到、上、回、在"等，介词如："从、在"等，后面常常有表示处所的宾语。如果宾语不是处所词，而是人称代词或指人指物的名词时，这些词后面一定要加"这儿"、"那儿"、"这里"或"那里"使之成为处所宾语。如："我从朋友那儿来"。不能说"我从朋友来"。"里"只能加在诸如"房子、礼堂、商店"这类兼指处所的名词后表示方位。"老师"是指人名词，不能加"里"，但是可以说"老师肚子里有很多学问"。

19. 你等她_____先看看报吧！

    A．这时                      B．那时

    C．这会儿                 D．那会儿

**题解**：正确答案是 C。"这会儿"有"这个时候"的意思，指现在或当前时刻，用在

某些词语后,表示当前这一确定的时间。"那会儿"则指过去或将来,根据句意应排除。"这时"、"那时"常放于句首。放于句中时,前后需用逗号隔开。

20. 他怎么_____爱挑毛病?
   A. 这么              B. 什么
   C. 多么              D. 要么

**题解**:"爱挑毛病"的意思是喜欢找别人的缺点或者缺陷。这是一个谓词性的结构,他的前边需要有一个状语。正确答案是 A。"这么"常用于形容词或表示心理活动的动词前,表程度,在句中做状语。"什么"是指代事物的疑问代词,不能做状语,"多么"虽也是一个程度副词,但只用于感叹句中,不可用于表反问句中,"要么"是一个表选择关系的连词。

21. 从这儿到火车站有_____五六十里地。
   A. 那些              B. 那么
   C. 那里              D. 这些

**题解**:正确答案是 B。"那么"可放在概数词前,表估计,此时应轻读。如"我们班有那么几个人对语法很有兴趣"。"这些、那些"是指代事物的,它们本身包含量的概念在里边,所以后边不能再有数量词语。"那里"是指代方位处所的,也应该排除。

22. 虽然《平凡的世界》也存在_____的缺点,但它的确是一部旷世杰作。
   A. 这么或那么         B. 这样或那样
   C. 这些或那些         D. 这里或那里

**题解**:正确答案是 B。"这么或那么"修饰谓词性成分,首先排除;"这些或那些"、"这样或那样"、"这里或那里"都可以修饰体词,但意义和用法有区别。"这些或那些"做修饰语后边不加"的",也可以排除;"这样或那样"做修饰语时后边必须加"的",符合条件。"这里或那里"指代处所,不符合题意,应排除。

23. 你在家等着,我马上出发_____。
   A. 去你这儿           B. 来你那儿
   C. 来你那儿           D. 去你那儿

**题解**:正确答案是 D。"去"是指"从说话人所在的地方到别的地方","别的地方"应用远指代词"那里/那儿"来指称,即应为"去……那儿";"来"正相反,是指从别的地方到说话人所在的地方,应用近指代词"这里/这儿"来指称,即应为"来……这儿",因此只有 D 是正确的。

24. 全国_____民族紧密团结在一起。
   A. 每                B. 各
   C. 每个              D. 每一个

**题解**:正确答案是 B。"每"要跟量词或数量词结合才能加在名词前,如"每本书,每个学生"(有"人、家"等少数例外),所以 A 可排除;另外,"每个"看重于取出一个或一组做例子,"各"指某个范围内的所有个体,侧重于同时遍指。根据题意应选 B,"各民族"指"全国"范围内的所有民族。"每个民族"指任何一个民族。

25. ＿＿＿＿＿＿地读者纷纷来信。

  A. 每           B. 各
  C. 到处          D. 各个

**题解**:正确答案是 B。"每"后需有量词或数量词才能加在名词前,如"每个家庭,每棵树"(有"人、家"等少数例外),所以 A 可排除。"到处"是副词不可做定语。"各个"不能修饰单音节名词,只有选 B。另外,"各地"、"各省"、"各民族"、"各学校"都是经常性的搭配,指某一范围内的全体。

26. 这里销售的＿＿＿＿＿＿本书都有作者签名。

  A. 每          B. 各
  C. 每个          D. 各个

**题解**:正确答案是 A。"一本"本身是数量结构,前边不需再加量词,C、D 可以排除。"各"做指示代词可以放于量词前,但不能用于数量结构前,故 B 应排除。"每"在句子中经常和"都"共现,表示周遍意义。选 A 是正确的。

27. 我＿＿＿＿＿＿都在想念着他。

  A. 每时每刻        B. 各时各刻
  C. 一时一刻        D. 时刻时刻

**题解**:正确答案是 A。"每"指的是全体中任何一个个体,在用"每"的句子里,常用表范围的副词"都"来强调,"时、刻"都是准量词,前可加"每"。"每时每刻"熟语性很强,而"各时各刻"没有熟语性,也就是说,我们从来不说"各时各刻"。"时刻"的重叠形式是"时时刻刻",不是"时刻时刻",所以 B、D 可以排除。"一时一刻"没有周遍意义,也可以排除。

28. ＿＿＿＿＿＿我看见天边的晚霞,就会想起童年的你。

  A. 当时          B. 各时
  C. 每时          D. 每当

**题解**:正确答案是 D。"每"做副词,表示同一动作,有规律地反复出现,后面常跟"逢、当、到"等。"各"不具有这种用法。"当时"指过去的某一具体时间,如果句子中的动作或行为是一次性出现的,我们可以说"当时我看见天边的彩霞,就想起了童年的你",但是这个句子的行为动作是反复出现的,所以应选择"每当"。

29. 心中的＿＿＿＿＿＿一个角落都深深刻着你的名字。

  A. 每          B. 各
  C. 每每          D. 各各

**题解**:正确答案是 A。理由同 27 题。"一个"本身是数量结构,不能用强调同一动作有规律地反复出现的"每每"和表示周遍意义的"各各"来修饰,故 C、D 可以排除。"各"做指示代词可以放在量词前,但不能用在数量结构前,故 B 应排除。"每"在句子中经常和"都"共现,表示周遍意义。选 A 是正确的。

30. _____到夏天,他就去海边度假。
   A. 各  B. 每
   C. 各个  D. 每个

**题解:** 正确答案是 B。"每"做副词,表示同一动作有规律地反复出现,后面常跟"逢、当、到"等。"各"不具有这种用法。"各个"、"每个"是因为有量词"个",所以后边应该是名词性成分,这里"到夏天"是谓词性成分,所以 C、D 可以排除。

31. _____年轻人盲目地加入了追星族的行列。
   A. 有些  B. 有的些
   C. 有些的  D. 有的一些

**题解:** 正确答案是 A。"些"是部分量词,"有些"指某一范围内的一部分。"些"前面或后面都不能直接加"的",所以"有的些"和"有些的"都不可接受。"有的"也指某一范围内的一部分,所以"有的"和"一些"连用语义重复,故 D 也是不可接受的。

32. 除了这几本书,还有_____吗?
   A. 多余  B. 其余
   C. 别的  D. 剩余

**题解:** 正确答案是 C。"别的"是旁指性代词,可做宾语,可以放在"有"后。A、B、D 没有"的",所以不可做宾语。

33. 教室里就你自己,没有_____吗?
   A. 谁  B. 其他
   C. 另外  D. 别人

**题解:** 正确答案是 D。"别人"是旁指性代词,用于泛指,指"除了某人之外的其他人"。"另外"和"其他"不加"的"或名词性成分不能单独做宾语。"谁"是疑问代词,"吗"是疑问语气词,二者都表示疑问,所以不能共现。

**副词**

34. 像她_____勤劳、美丽、善良的人实在难得。
   A. 这些  B. 那里
   C. 那些  D. 那么

**题解:** 正确答案是 D。"那么"可放在形容词前表示程度,如"天那么冷,他竟然不穿棉衣"。"这些"、"那些"是指代事物的,它们应该修饰名词时,不能修饰形容词,应该排除;"那里"是指代方位处所的,也不能修饰形容词,所以应该排除。

35. 这几天我忙得连报纸都_____了。
   A. 不看成   B. 看不成
   C. 不阅成   D. 阅不成

   **题解**：正确答案是 B。在汉语中，"动词+不+谓词性成分(形容词、动词、趋向动词)"是一个典型的述补结构，是动词的可能态，表示主观能力达不到或客观条件不允许。比如"举不起"、"听不清"、"看不见"。所以 A、C 从形式上可以排除。"阅"是一个不成词语素，故排除。

36. 这本书我实在_____。
   A. 看不进去   B. 不看进去
   C. 不进去看   D. 看进不去

   **题解**：正确答案是 A。理由同上。在汉语中，"动词+不+谓词性成分(形容词、动词、趋向动词)"是一个典型的述补结构，是动词的可能态，表示主观能力达不到或客观条件不允许。比如"拿不出来"、"抬不进去"、"看不出来"、"干不下去"等，这样从形式上可以排除"不看进去"和"不进去看"。"进不去"是个合格的语法形式，但是前边如果再有动词性成分就应该是"V不进去"，而没有"V进不去"。

37. 他十分骄傲，从来就_____。
   A. 看不起别人   B. 不看起别人
   C. 不别人看起   D. 别人不看起

   **题解**：正确答案是 A。这是一种特殊的可能补语，与上述类型的可能补语相比，它没有相应的肯定形式，如"来不及——＊来及"、"对不起——＊对起"、"看不起——＊看起"。这类可能补语多与前边的动词结合很紧，形成一个熟语性结构，如"看不起"的意思是"轻视"，"对不起"的意思是"对人有愧"。既然没有"＊看起"这个形式，所以 B、C、D 都可以排除。

**动词**

38. 我小时候_____。
   A. 写过用毛笔字   B. 写用过毛笔字
   C. 写过字用毛笔字   D. 写过毛笔字

   **题解**：正确答案是 D。动态助词"过"接在动词后表示曾经有过某种经历，后边可以带体词宾语。如果出现工具格("用+工具名词")，工具格必须出现在动词之前，否则就不能使用工具格。这几个选择除了 D 之外工具格都出现在动词之后，所以 A、B、C 都是错的。

39. 每天下午我们都在操场上_____两小时球。
   A. 打   B. 打打
   C. 打一打   D. 打了打

   **题解**：正确答案是 A。B、C、D 都是动词"打"的重叠形式，表动作相对时间短或相对次数少,动作持续的时间长短是不确定的,而题中有"每天下午"和"两小时"的限制,时间长短很确定,故只能选 A。

40. 明天上午我们一起去_____世界公园。
    A. 看望　　　　　　　　　　B. 访问
    C. 参观　　　　　　　　　　D. 旅游

**题解**:正确答案是 C。D"旅游"是一个不及物动词,应该首先排除;而 A 后只能跟表人的宾语,B 后的宾语可以是人、城市、国家等(有人来代表它们接受访问,它们在修辞上可以拟人化),但不能是公共场所。"参观"的对象可以是公共场所,所以选 C。

41. 他_____绿茶。
    A. 爱喝最　　　　　　　　　B. 最爱喝
    C. 喝最爱　　　　　　　　　D. 爱最喝

**题解**:正确答案是 B。"爱"是表示人的精神、心理活动的动词,可以带体词性宾语,如"爱孩子";也可以带谓词性宾语,如"爱听音乐"。如果有表示程度的副词做"爱"的修饰语,必须放在它的前边,不能放在它的后边,如"最爱听音乐"可以说,但是"爱听最音乐"、"爱最听音乐"都不能接受,所以 A、D 应该排除;表示极端的程度副词"最"修饰"爱"以后,前边不能有谓词性成分,C 应排除。所以只有"最爱喝绿茶"是正确的。

42. 他侧耳_____,什么也没听见。
    A. 听　　　　　　　　　　　B. 听一听
    C. 听不听　　　　　　　　　D. 听了听

**题解**:正确答案是 D。这里"听"是一个已发生的动作,因为下文有"没听见","听"单独使用没有时间标志,不能判断是过去、现在、还是未来,它所指涉(denote)的过程前后都没有界限,用在这里意思含糊,故应该排除;"听一听"是表示将要发生的动作,也应该排除;"听不听"表示疑问,与下文不一致,所以只有选 D,"听了听"表示已经完结的动作。

43. 他_____游泳。
    A. 非常喜欢　　　　　　　　B. 喜欢非常
    C. 喜喜欢欢　　　　　　　　D. 喜欢喜欢

**题解**:正确答案是 A,"喜欢"是一个动词,副词做修饰语必须放在动词之前,所以排除了 B"喜欢非常";另外,"喜欢"在汉语中无重叠形式,C"喜喜欢欢"和 D"喜欢喜欢"都不成立。只有 A 正确。

44. 老师_____批评。
    A. 正在进行对她　　　　　　B. 正在对她进行
    C. 对她进行正在　　　　　　D. 进行正在对她

**题解**:正确答案是 B。"进行"是一个谓宾动词,后边必须接一个谓词性宾语,如果有介词结构或者副词做状语修饰"进行",必须放在"进行"的前边,"对她"和

"正在"都是介词结构做状语,都应该放在"进行"之前。所以 A、C、D 都是错的。

45. 他_____大学。

  A．希望了明年考上      B．明年希望考上了

  C．希望明年能考上      D．明年能希望考上

**题解**:正确答案是 C。"希望"是一个只能带谓词性宾语(verbal objects)的动词,它的谓词性宾语常常是一个主谓结构,"明年能考上大学"是一个主谓结构,故选 C。"希望"是一个不能加"了"的动词,所以 A 是错的;"希望"所带的谓词宾语也不能是经历态或完结态,B 的"考上了"是完结态,因而也是错的;"希望"不能受"能"、"愿意"、"乐意"这样的助动词修饰,因此 D 也是错的。

46. 张明知道那件事,可以让他给我_____。

  A．说了说        B．一说说

  C．说一说        D．就说说

**题解**:正确答案是 C。"可以让他给我做什么"是将来要发生的事,所以不能用表示完结和实现的重叠形式"说了说",A 可以排除;动词重叠以后不能受"一"的修饰,因为"一+动词"表示动作的尝试态,不能持续,不能重复,而动词重叠以后虽然表示动作短时少量,但动作有持续进行特征,且可以重复,在时间上必须有一个过程。B "一说说"在语法上不能成立。C "说一说"表示的是将要发生的事,与题意吻合。D "给我就说说"语法上也不成立,因为"给我"和"就"都是状语,按照汉语多重状语排列的顺序,副词应该排在介词结构前边,也就是说,我们可以说"就给我说说",但是不能说"给我就说说"。

47. 这个问题很难,我们一起_____吧。

  A．研究一研究       B．研究了研究

  C．研究研究        D．研研究究

**题解**:正确答案是 C。这里动词"研究"是一个双音节动词,它的重叠形式是"AB — ABAB"式。所以 D 首先可以排除;双音节动词的重叠形式没有"AB — AB",故 A "研究一研究"可以排除;"研究了研究"因为有"了",表达的是动作的完结态,而句中"一起……吧"显然是祈使句,与完结态矛盾,这样 B 也被排除了。

48. 一个优秀学生,既_____学习好,又_____品行好。

  A．会……会        B．能……能

  C．想……想        D．要……要

**题解**:正确答案是 D。这里"要"表示事实上或情理上的需要,意思是"应该",用于未然的情况。"会"、"能"都表示能力许可或条件允许,"想"的意思是"打算",表达的是一种愿望,它们与"一个优秀学生应该怎么样"的题意不符。

49. 成功是_____得到的。

　　A. 不要轻易　　　　　　　　　　B. 轻易不要

　　C. 不轻易会　　　　　　　　　　D. 不会轻易

**题解**：正确答案是 D。"不要"表禁止或"不必要"，A、B 可以排除；"轻易"是"得到"的修饰成分，不是"会"的修饰成分，所以 C 也可以排除。"不会"表推测，意思是"不可能"，故选 D。

## 助动词

50. 太晚了，估计_____了。

　　A. 不会他来　　　　　　　　　　B. 不能他来

　　C. 他不会来　　　　　　　　　　D. 他来不能

**题解**：正确答案是 C。"估计"是一个必须带谓词性宾语的谓宾动词，除非做插入语，通常应该带一个整句做宾语，"他不会来了"是一个很好的整句，所以可以放在"估计"后。另外，助动词必须直接放在谓词性成分前，中间不能插入别的成分，所以 A、B、D 均可排除。

51. 小王，我_____你的自行车吗？

　　A. 用　　　　　　　　　　　　　B. 要用

　　C. 会用　　　　　　　　　　　　D. 能用

**题解**：正确答案是 D。这是一个征求对方意见的疑问句，需用表示"准许"与否的助动词，没有助动词的"用"应首先排除，只有"能"表示主观允许或客观许可；而"要"、"会"表示的是可能性或打算等，没有"许可"这种意味，故选 D。

52. 把你的钢笔借给我用一下，_____吗？

　　A. 可能　　　　　　　　　　　　B. 可以

　　C. 应该　　　　　　　　　　　　D. 会

**题解**：这是一个征询对方许可的疑问句。A"可能"表示估计，意思是"也许"、"或许"；C"应该"表示情理上必须如此；D"会"表示客观可能性或主观能力。只有 B"可以"表示许可，故选 B。

53. 请问，这儿_____吸烟？

　　A. 能不能　　　　　　　　　　　B. 要不要

　　C. 会不会　　　　　　　　　　　D. 可能不可能

**题解**：正确答案是 A。这是一个疑问句，问是否允许吸烟，答案中只有 A"能不能"表示"许可不许可"的意思，B"要不要"是"应该不应该"、"需要不需要"的意思；C"会不会"是询问可能性，或是否有做某事的能力，D"可能不可能"也是询问可能性，都不合题意。

54. 老师要求这篇作文星期一就_____交上来。
    A. 想                              B. 得
    C. 会                              D. 愿意

**题解**：正确答案是 B。"得"，音 děi，上声，表示情理上需要，比"应该"语气更肯定，而且更口语化；"想"、"愿意"都表示主观上的意愿；"会"表示客观可能性或主观能力。可见只有 B 符合题意。

55. 这本书_____借给我吗？
    A. 可以能                          B. 会可以
    C. 能会                            D. 能

**题解**：正确答案是 D。"能"、"会"都是助动词，尽管汉语语法中某些助动词可以连用，但"可以"、"能"、"会"都可表可能性，用在一起会导致意义上的重复。所以 A、B、C 都应该排除。

56. 你_____我这儿来一趟？
    A. 能到不到                        B. 能不能到
    C. 能到不能                        D. 到能不能

**题解**：正确答案是 B。助动词的语法特征之一是能用肯定否定并列的方式（如"能不能"、"会不会"、"要不要"等）表示选择疑问，这是一个选择疑问句，只有 B 符合要求。助动词的语法特征之二是做修饰语时只能放在动词或谓词性结构前，所以 D 是错的；助动词的语法特征之三是它不能带宾语，所以 C 可以排除。这个句子是询问可能性的，所以肯定否定并列的应该是"能"，而不应该是"到"，所以 A 也不对。

57. 他_____迷了路？
    A. 要不要                          B. 会不会
    C. 可能不                          D. 可以不

**题解**：正确答案是 B。根据题意可知这是一个选择疑问句，应该用肯定否定并列的形式来表达，所以首先排除 C、D。A"要不要"的意思是"是否打算"、"是否应该"，与题意不符，应该排除；"会不会"是询问客观可能性或主观上是否具有某种能力，根据题意应该选 B。

58. 你_____交给他吗？
    A. 把信可以                        B. 把信能不能
    C. 把信能                          D. 能把信

**题解**：正确答案是 D。这是一个是非疑问句，中间包孕一个"把"字结构。是非疑问句有疑问语气词"吗"做标记，因此不能用选择疑问形式"能不能"，排除 B；助动词和否定副词在"把"字结构中必须放在"把"字之前，所以 A、C 都是错的。

59. 还有一个小时,你_____完成作业?
   A. 可不可以                B. 可以不可以
   C. 能不能                  D. 要不要

题解:正确答案是 C。C"能不能"表示主观上是否有某种能力或客观上是否有某种可能性,A"可不可以"和 B"可以不可以"都表示客观条件是不是允许,D"要不要"的意思是"是否打算"、"是否应该",根据题意,选 C。

60. 你没有钱,就_____娶我女儿。
   A. 不会                    B. 不想
   C. 不要                    D. 不行

题解:正确答案是 C。"要"是助动词,表示打算,应该。否定用"不要",表示禁止或劝阻。句中题意正是表示禁止、劝阻;A"不会"是对"可能性"的否定,B"不想"是主观上不愿意。D"不行"只能做谓语中心成分,不能用来做其他谓词性结构的状语。根据题意,选 C。

61. 我们_____活着。
   A. 无忧无虑地可以          B. 可以无忧无虑地
   C. 无忧无虑地可能          D. 可能无忧无虑地

题解:正确答案是 B。这里"无忧无虑地"做"活着"的状语,修饰限制"活着",而"可以"是助动词,在这里做"无忧无虑地活着"的状语,修饰限制的是"无忧无虑地活着"。"可能"是副词,表示估计,与题意不合,所以 C、D 应排除;"无忧无虑地"是状态词性质的,"可以"是助动词,在做状语的时候,"助动词"应该在状态词前,所以 A 应该排除。故选 B。

62. 经理答应了,你_____谈一谈。
   A. 跟他可能                B. 跟他会
   C. 可以跟他                D. 会跟他

题解:正确答案是 C。根据"经理答应了"我们知道,"谈一谈"前需要一个表"许可"或"建议"的助动词,只有 C 符合条件,因为"可以"有"许可"的意思。"可能"和"会"都表示估计,与题意不合,所以排除 A、B、D。

63. 你妈妈_____嫁给他吗?
   A. 同意你能                B. 能你同意
   C. 同意能你                D. 能同意你

题解:正确答案是 D。这是一个包孕句,又是一个疑问句,询问可能性,主要结构是"你妈妈……同意……吗?""同意"的宾语是一个子句"你嫁给他",助动词"能"应该放在主要动词"同意"前,因此排除了 A、B、C。故选 D。

64. 今天作业太多,晚会我_____参加了。
   A. 不可以                  B. 不能
   C. 不要                    D. 不应该

题解:正确答案是 B。从"今天作业太多"我们知道后边的分句一定是表示可能性或意愿的,A"不可以"的意思是"不许可",是禁止的意思,与题意不合;B"不能"的意思是主观能力或客观条件不许可,与题意正好契合,故选 B。C"不要"表禁止或劝阻,不合题意。D"不应该"表示在情理上不好,不表示可能或意愿,可以排除。

65. 以后我们_____更加努力学习。

  A. 一定要         B. 要一定

  C. 一定应该        D. 应该一定

**题解**:正确答案是 A。助动词可以受副词修饰,但是不同的助动词情况不同。"一定"可以修饰"要",不能修饰"应该",所以排除了 C;另外,"一定"是副词,必须放于助动词前,因而排除了 B 和 D。

66. 我见到他的时候,他_____一件大衣

  A. 正会买去商店       B. 正会去商店买

  C. 正要去商店买       D. 正要买去商店

**题解**:正确答案是 C。"会"的意思是:(1)懂得做或有能力做某事(2)善于做某事(3)有可能。而"要"的意思是"将要"、"打算",根据题意,此处谓语表示的是主语的打算,故可排除 A、B。从另一个角度看,这个句子有三个题元(arguments):"他"、"商店"、"一件大衣",谓项(predicates)有"去"和"买",助动词"要"或者修饰"去",或者修饰"买",或者修饰"去……买",不可能修饰"买去",所以应该排除 D;"去"的宾语是"商店","买"的宾语是"一件大衣","要"修饰的是"去……买",这样看只有 C 符合条件。

67. 他_____学会开汽车。

  A. 想想          B. 想

  C. 想一想         D. 想了想

**题解**:正确答案是 B。这个句子的"学会开汽车"是谓词性的,所以空白的地方应该填上助动词。助动词不能重叠,所以 A、C、D 都可排除。

### "的"字结构

68. _____喜欢漂亮女友,_____喜欢有钱男友。

  A. 男……女        B. 男的……女的

  C. 男的人……女的人     D. 有的男……有的女

**题解**:正确答案是 B。名词、代词、形容词、动词、主谓短语、区别词等都可以加"的"构成"的"字短语,功能相当于一个名词。"男"、"女"是区别词,不能单独做主宾语,加上"的"以后变成名词才能做主宾语,因此我们可以排除 A、D;"男的"、"女的"是分类性的,只能用于人类,所以不需特意指明"男的人"、"女的人",这样也就排除了 C。

69. 人到中年上有_____下有_____,负担很重。
　　A. 老的……小的　　　　　　　B. 大……小
　　C. 老人……小人　　　　　　　D. 大人……小人

题解:正确答案是 A。在汉语里,"小人"有特定的意义,它与"君子"是相对的,古时候指地位低的人,现在指人格卑鄙的人,不能望文生义地把"小人"理解为"年幼的人",故 C、D 可以排除。另外,在年龄这个顺序义场中,与"中年"相对应的是:"老年"(简称"老")、"青年"、"少年"、"儿童"(简称"小"),由此可见,"老的"、"小的"是指称性的,指特定年龄段的人,而"大"、"小"只是相对年龄,故可以排除 B。"上有老的、下有小的"是汉语中一个惯用说法。

70. 听他这样一说,她的脸_____。
　　A. 红红的　　　　　　　　　　B. 红红了
　　C. 红了　　　　　　　　　　　D. 红的了

题解:正确答案是 C。单音节形容词的重叠形式不能单独做谓语,后面要加上"的"(变成 AA 的)才可以;形容词重叠以后表示一种状态,有程度的含义在内,因此排斥结果意义很强的"了",故 B 不能成立。A 和 D 中的"的"是结构助词,"红的"是一个"的"字结构,功能上相当于一个名词,所以不能单独做谓语,也不能带动态助词"了"。所以 A 和 D 也都不能成立。

**形容词**

71. 请大家_____,我们现在开始上课。
　　A. 安一安静　　　　　　　　　B. 安静安静
　　C. 安安静静　　　　　　　　　D. 安静一静

题解:正确答案是 B。"安静"是一个动词和形容词兼类的词,按动词重叠方式重叠应该是"安静安静"(ABAB 式),按形容词重叠方式重叠应该是"安安静静"(AABB 式)。这里"安静"应该是一个动词,所以可以排除 C,选择 B;A、D 都是不合语法规则的形式,也应该排除。

72. 给小妹戴上项链,让她也_____。
　　A. 漂亮漂亮　　　　　　　　　B. 非常漂亮的
　　C. 漂漂亮亮　　　　　　　　　D. 很漂亮

题解:正确答案是 A。"漂亮"用法同"安静",也是一个动词和形容词兼类的词。作为形容词重叠以后加"的"方可做谓语成分,但重叠式本身却不能做谓语,因此排除了 C。形容词重叠以后不能接受程度副词"很、非常"等词的修饰,因此排除 B;这个句子中的"让"有"使令"义,它要求后边的谓词性成分是表示变化或结果的,不能是表示程度的,所以不能用 D"很漂亮"。

73. 他背起书包，_____上学去了。
    A. 很高高兴兴　　　　　　　　B. 高兴
    C. 高兴高兴　　　　　　　　　D. 高高兴兴

题解：正确答案是 D。"高兴"用法同"安静"、"漂亮"。此处做状语,应采用形容词的重叠式 AABB;形容词重叠以后有程度意义在内,表示程度深,所以前面不再加程度副词,排除 A。另外,双音节形容词在口语里很少单独做状语,有些做状语时,后面需加"地",所以排除 B。此处应选 D。

74. 他们把教室打扫得_____。
    A. 干净　　　　　　　　　　　B. 干净干净
    C. 干干净净　　　　　　　　　D. 很干干净净

题解：正确答案是 C。"干净"是形容词,此处做"得"后的补语,表示结果,应该用形容词的重叠式 AABB 式,因此排除了 A、B;形容词重叠以后不能再受程度副词修饰,因此 D 也被排除了。

75. 我们要_____举爱国主义的旗帜。
    A. 高高　　　　　　　　　　　B. 很高
    C. 高　　　　　　　　　　　　D. 高的

题解：正确答案是 C。根据音节搭配的音便原则,单音节形容词通常放在单音节动词前做修饰语,如"高呼"、"高喊"、"大干"、"快上"等,双音节形容词通常放在双音节动词或动词词组前做修饰语(祈使句例外),如"顽固抵抗"、"坚决抵制"、"成功发射"、"光荣退休"等。这个例子中的动词是单音节动词"举",因此选 C。但是请注意:不是所有的形容词都能出现在动词或动词结构前做修饰语。

76. 别东张西望的，_____听课！
    A. 好　　　　　　　　　　　　B. 很好
    C. 好好　　　　　　　　　　　D. 好一好

题解：正确答案是 C。"听课"是一个双音节的动词性结构,根据音节搭配的音便原则,"听课"前应该加双音节形容词做修饰语,"好"是一单音节性质形容词,故排除。单音节性质形容词重叠后可做状语,"好好"合乎条件;祈使句中的形容词重叠形式做状语都是表示祈使意义的,如"慢慢说"、"好好干"、"狠狠打他"等。"很好"是一个陈述结构,不能用在祈使句中,故 B 不合适;"好一好"是一个错误搭配,因为没有 A—A 的结构形式。

**数量词**

77. 我们学校有_____名学生。
    A. 两千两百两十两　　　　　　B. 两千二百二十二
    C. 二千两百二十两　　　　　　D. 二千二百两十二

**题解**：正确答案是 B。"二"和"两"都代表"2"，但用法不一样。位数词"十、百、千、万、亿"只有"十、百"前要用"二"，而"千、万、亿"前通常用"两"。系位组合的末项也必须用"二"，如"十二"、"一百零二"、"三百二"。所以只有 B 符合这个要求。

78. 我昨天看了_____小说。

　　A．三个半小时　　　　　　　　B．三个小时半
　　C．三小时半个　　　　　　　　D．半个三小时

**题解**：正确答案是 A。"半"做数词时，可以放在量词前，也可以放在量词后，但是如果和其他数词一起出现，则必须采用"其他数词 + 量词 + 半 +（名词）"的顺序。上面四个答案只有 A 符合这一要求。

79. 参加集会的有_____人。

　　A．三万四千九百六十　　　　　B．三万零四千九百六十
　　C．三万四千九百零六十　　　　D．三万四千零九百六十

**题解**：正确答案是 A。"零"做数词时用来表示数的空位，在数的表达中，如果出现位数词空档，用"零"代替。如 30235 是"三万零二百三十五"，23022 是"两万三千零二十二"。"三万四千九百六十"是 34960，在这个选项里十位以上的位数词都没有空档，因此不必用"零"去填空。

80. 我是_____的学生。

　　A．大学二年级　　　　　　　　B．大学两年级
　　C．二年级大学　　　　　　　　D．两年级大学

**题解**：正确答案是 A。这里涉及到两个问题：一个是"两"和"二"的使用问题，一个是语序问题。序数、分数、小数前只能用"二"。比如"二年级"、"二分之一"、"二点五"等，不能用"两"，因此排除了 B、D。C 的语序不符合汉语从大到小的表达规则，"大学"和"二年级"应该把"大学"放在前面，"二年级"放在后面。

81. 从这里_____到西直门下车。

　　A．乘汽车 375 路　　　　　　　B．汽车 375 路乘
　　C．375 路汽车乘　　　　　　　D．乘 375 路汽车

**题解**：正确答案是 D。汉语的宾语和动词的位置关系是动词在宾语前，所以 B、C 两个答案肯定是错的。另外，汉语中定语和中心语的关系也是定语在前，中心语在后，"375 路"是"汽车"的定语，所以"375 路汽车"是合法搭配，"汽车 375 路"不是合法的搭配，因此 A 也不对。

82. 我住在北露园小区_____。

　　A．15 号 6 门 14 楼　　　　　　B．6 门 15 号 14 楼
　　C．14 楼 6 门 15 号　　　　　　D．14 楼 15 号 6 门

**题解**：正确答案是 C。中国人的表达习惯是从大到小，因此应按"楼、门、号"的前

后顺序来表达。这样,只有C才对。

83. 这封信的发出日期是_____。

  A. 1934年4日8月      B. 4月8日1934年

  C. 8日4月1934年      D. 1934年8月4日

题解:正确答案是D。中国人的表达习惯是从大到小,因此应按"年、月、日"的前后顺序来表达。这样,只有D才对。

84. 他们的房间里有_____书架。

  A. 二个          B. 两个

  C. 二           D. 两

题解:这是一个"二"和"两"的用法区别的问题,正确答案是B。汉语的数词后应该有量词,所以C、D可排除。量词"个"前数词要用"两",不能用"二"。故选B。

85. 今天我们买书花了_____。

  A. 两十五块两毛二      B. 二十五块二毛两

  C. 二十五块两毛二      D. 两十五块二毛二

题解:这是一个"二"和"两"的用法区别的问题,正确答案是C。"二"和"两"都代表"2",但用法不一样。位数词"十、百、千、万、亿"中只有"十、百"前要用"二",而"千、万、亿"前通常用"两"。系位组合的末项也必须用"二",如"十二"、"一百零二"、"三百二"。所以只有C符合这个要求。

86. 那所学校有_____人。

  A. 十五千多        B. 十五多千

  C. 一万五多千       D. 一万五千多

题解:正确答案是D。汉语的基数词分为系数词与位数词两种:例如整数的系数词是:一、二、三、四、五、六、七、八、九、十等;位数词是:十、百、千、万、亿等;其中"十"既是系数词又是位数词。汉语按十进制计算法计数,数目在万以下时,系数词不超过"十",超过"十"后应往前进一位,因此不能说"十五千",应说"一万五千"。这样就排除了A、B两个选择。"多"表示概数时只能放在位数词之后,如"二百多","两万多",不说"二多百","两多万"。因此只有D是正确的。

87. 他旷课已经_____了。

  A. 十四几天        B. 十四五天

  C. 十几天多        D. 十五四天

题解:正确答案是B。两个相邻的数词连用,表示概数。连用的一般为系数词,通常数目小的在前,大的在后,如"八九个"、"十五六个",这就排除了D。"九"和"十"不能连用表示概数。和"几"连用表示概数的数词仅限于如"十几天"、"二十几年"等十以上、百以下的整数,而不能是"五几天"、"十四几天"这样的非整数,所以A也是错的。"十几"已经是表示概数的了,"多"也是表示概数的,放在一起显得重复,因此 C 也是错的。

88. 这个电影院坐得下_____人。

  A. 五百六百　　　　　　　　　B. 五六多百

  C. 五六百多　　　　　　　　　D. 五六百

题解:正确答案是 D。十以上的整数要连用表示概数,两个相邻的数词连用以后,后边接一个位数词就可以了,如"五六百"、"六七百",不用"五百六百",因此 A 不对。连用的数词也是数目小的在前,大的在后,如"八九十"、"五六百",只有 D 符合这个条件。基数词连用已经能够表示概数了,"多"也是表示概数的,放在一起显得重复,因此 B、C 也是错的。

89. 她_____没收到他的信了。

  A. 三个月多　　　　　　　　　B. 三多个月

  C. 三个多月　　　　　　　　　D. 三月多个

题解:正确答案是 C。"多"用在数量词后表示不确定的零数。它的位置及用法是:(1)数词 + 多 + 量词( + 名词),这里的数词必须是 10 以上(包括"十")的整数,如"十多斤(苹果)"、"一百多个(学生)",四个答案显然都不属于这种用法;(2)数词 + 量词 + 多( + 名词),这里的数词必须是从 1 到 10 的基数词(包括"两")。这里的四个答案只有 C 符合条件。

90. 她一顿饭吃了_____。

  A. 两多小时　　　　　　　　　B. 两个多小时

  C. 两多个小时　　　　　　　　D. 两小时个多

题解:正确答案是 B。"多"用在数量词后表示不确定的零数。它的位置及用法是:(1)数词 + 多 + 量词( + 名词),但在这种用法中数词必须是 10 以上(包括"十")的整数,如"十多斤(苹果)"、"一百多个(学生)",四个答案显然都不符合这个条件;(2)数词 + 量词 + 多( + 名词),这里的数词必须是从 1 到 10 的基数词(包括"两")。这里的四个答案只有 B 符合条件。

91. 他有_____美国朋友。

  A. 几　　　　　　　　　　　　B. 几个

  C. 几多　　　　　　　　　　　D. 几人

题解:正确答案是 B。"几"作为一个概数词在表示不定数目时,除了问年龄(例如"他二十几了?")外,后面都要有量词或用为临时量词的名词(例如"几天"、"几年")。A 和 C 没有量词,排除出去;D 中的"人"在这里不是量词,也不是临时量词,所以也可以排除出去。

92. 9号楼住着_____中国学生。

  A. 几十五个　　　　　　　　　B. 几十个

  C. 几十个多　　　　　　　　　D. 几十多个

**题解:** 正确答案是 B。"几"可以在数列中代替系数词,表示 10(不包括 10)以下的概数,比如"十几本书"、"几十个人"、"几百人",与"几"连用的数词只能是表示整数的位数词(如"十"、"百"、"千"等),A 的"十五"不是整数,不符合这个条件;"多"本身也是表概数的,不再用在概数词后,所以 C、D 也不对。

93. 我们班有_____的人参加了比赛。
   A. 二分之三  B. 二三之分
   C. 三分之二  D. 三二分之

**题解:** 正确答案是 C。分数通常的说法是"X 分之 Y","X"表示分母,后面的"Y"表示分子。例如 2/3 读成"三分之二"。因此 B 和 D 都是错的;A 没有语法上的问题,我们可以说"二分之三"(3/2),但是在这个句子里所表达的意思与常识不符,一个班不可能有 3/2 个人,所以也是错的。

94. 这种药品的总有效率达到_____。
   A. 百分之九十八点三十五  B. 百分九十八点之三五
   C. 百分九十八之三五  D. 百分之九十八点三五

**题解:** 这是一个分数和小数读法的问题,正确答案是 D。百分数的表达法是"百分之 X",B、C 都不符合这个条件。小数部分通常的说法是把小数点读作"点",小数点以后的部分只读系数词,如"3.1416"读作"三点一四一六",因此 A 是错的。只有 D 符合这个条件。

95. 我刚才吃了_____梨。
   A. 半  B. 半一个
   C. 半个  D. 一半个

**题解:** 正确答案是 C。无整数时,数词"半"用在量词前,如"半斤"、"半个"、"半尺";有整数时,"半"用在量词后,后面再接名词,名词可以省去。如"一斤半(肉)"、"一里半(地)"。A 没有量词,B 和 D 都多用了一个数词"一",只有 C 正确。

96. 我到北京_____了。
   A. 已经三年半  B. 已经三半年
   C. 三年半已经  D. 半三年已经

**题解:** 正确答案是 A。无整数时,数词"半"用在量词前,如"半斤"、"半个"、"半尺";有整数时,"半"用在量词后,后面再接名词,名词可以省去。如"一斤半(肉)"、"三里半(地)"、"四年半(时间)"。B、D 有整数"三",因此"半"应该放在"年"后,排除 B、D。此处"已经"做"三年半了"这个短语的状语,应该放在"三年半了"的前面,因此 C 也应当排除。

97. 这本书才_____。
   A. 五块五十五分  B. 五块零五十五分
   C. 五块五毛五  D. 五块零五毛零五分

**题解:** 正确答案是 C。中国现行货币人民币的单位是元(口语叫"块")、角(口语叫"毛")、分,10进制,10分等于1角(毛),10毛等于1元(块)。相邻的单位之间不用"零",如5.55元读做"五块五毛五",不读做"五块零五毛五",只有不相邻的单位之间才用"零",如5.05元要读做"五块零五分"。

98. 这本书才_____。

  A．五块五毛钱        B．五块零五十分

  C．五块五十分        D．五块零五毛钱

**题解**：正确答案是A。中国现行货币人民币的单位是元(口语叫"块")、角(口语叫"毛")、分,十进制,10分等于1角(毛),10毛等于1元(块)。相邻的单位之间不用"零",如5.55元读做"五块五毛五",不读做"五块零五毛五",只有不相邻的单位之间才用"零",如5.05元要读做"五块零五分"。所以B和D都是错的;因为是十进制,所以没有"五十分"的说法,C也是错的。

99. 这个月我付给你_____钱。

  A．五百十五块        B．五百一十五块

  C．五百一零十五块       D．五百一零五块

**题解**：正确答案是B。汉语中11～19的称数法是"十一,十二,……十八,十九";不必说"一十一,一十二……一十八,一十九","十"前边的"一"可以省略,但在三位数以上的数字中,"一"是不能省略的。如318应该读做"三百一十八",因此A是错的;"零"的用法是代替位数词中的空位,如308读做"三百零八",没有空位的时候不用"零",所以C、D也是错的。

### 量词

100. 那_____词典是小王的。

  A．张           B．把

  C．条           D．本

**题解**：正确答案是D。个体名词都有自己特定的个体量词。例如"书"论"本","床"论"张",名词和跟它相配的个体量词之间有的时候在意义上有某种联系。但这只是少数情况,什么名词用什么量词是约定俗成的。"词典"前可用"本",也可用"部"。

101. 我刚买了一_____蓝色夹克衫。

  A．个           B．张

  C．件           D．把

**题解**：正确答案是C。理由同上。有延展平面的东西论"张"。有把儿的东西一般论"把",上衣论"件"。

102. 三_____请里边坐。

  A．个           B．位

  C．名           D．人

**题解**：正确答案是B。理由同第100题。这四个量词都可以与指人名词搭配,但

使用在称呼语里的时候只能用"几位,您几位,你们三位",表示对被称呼者的尊敬和客气。

103. 这套房子有两_____卧室。
   A. 所                    B. 座
   C. 间                    D. 件

**题解:** 正确答案是 C。理由同上。"所"后一般与"学校"、"医院"等名词搭配;"座"与"房子"、"院落"、"工厂"、"山"等名词搭配,"件"与"衣服"、"礼物"、"事"等名词搭配。"间"与"屋子"、"卧室"等名词搭配。

104. 在我家的后院有两_____树。
   A. 课                    B. 条
   C. 棵                    D. 支

**题解:** 正确答案是 C。理由同上。"课"常与"课文"搭配,"条"一般用于长条形状的物体,"支"常与"笔"、"队伍"等名词搭配。"树"的量词是"棵"。

105. 池塘里有几_____鸭子。
   A. 位                    B. 张
   C. 条                    D. 只

**题解:** 正确答案是 D。"位"与表人的名词搭配,有延展平面的东西论"张",长条形状的物体论"条","鸭子"论"只"。

106. 我家一共有五_____人。
   A. 口                    B. 位
   C. 名                    D. 头

**题解:** 正确答案是 A。理由同 100 题。"口"作为量词,可以与"人"搭配,用来计数人口,还可以与"井"、"锅"等名词搭配,用来计数数量。"名"作为量词用于有某种身份的人之前。"头"作为量词,与"猪"或"大蒜"等名词搭配,"位"作为量词与表示人的名词如"客人"、"小姐"等搭配,有尊敬意味,但不能与"人"直接搭配。

107. 书房里放着两_____椅子。
   A. 位                    B. 把
   C. 条                    D. 件

**题解:** 正确答案是 B。"位"作为量词与表示人的名词如"客人"、"小姐"等搭配,有尊敬意味,"条"与长条状的物体或某些抽象名词如"意见"等搭配,"件"与"衣服"、"事"等名词搭配,"椅子"的量词是"把"。

108. 这些孩子_____聪明伶俐。
   A. 每个                  B. 每一个
   C. 个个                  D. 一个

**题解:**正确答案是 C。量词重叠表示"由个体组成的全体",或者说"表示周遍意义",有"毫无例外"的意思,可以做主语。"每个"和"每一个"指"全体中的个体",如果要表示"由个体组成的全体",则必须在其后用"都"来总括。"一个"只能表示个体。根据题意应选 C。

109. 红红的太阳照着孩子们那_____可爱的笑脸。

    A. 一张张  B. 一些张
    C. 每张张  D. 一张

**题解:**正确答案是 A。量词重叠表示"由个体组成的全体",或者说"表示周遍意义",有"毫无例外"的意思,重叠后可以受数词"一"且只能受"一"的修饰,所以选 A,排除 C。"孩子们……的笑脸"是复数,排除 D;"张"不能受"些"这个不定量词的修饰,排除 B。

110. _____大路通罗马。

    A. 每条  B. 条条
    C. 每一条  D. 所有条

**题解:**正确答案是 B。量词重叠表示"由个体组成的全体",或者说"表示周遍意义",有"毫无例外"的意思,可以做主语,也可以做定语。"每条"和"每一条"指"全体中的个体",如果要表示"由个体组成的全体"则必须在其后用"都"来总括。"所有"后边应该有名词,不能直接修饰量词"条"。另外,"条条大路通罗马"是一个熟语。

111. _____迹象表明,他这个人很虚伪。

    A. 每种  B. 每一种
    C. 种种  D. 每种种

**题解:**正确答案是 C。量词重叠表示"由个体组成的全体",或者说"表示周遍意义",有"毫无例外"的意思,可以做主语或定语。"每种"和"每一种"指"全体中的个体",如果要表示"由个体组成的全体",则必须在其后用"都"来总括,所以 A、B 可以排除。量词重叠以后不能受"每"修饰,D 也可以排除。

112. 他先后几_____去办公室找她。

    A. 遍  B. 次
    C. 下  D. 阵

**题解:**正确答案是 B。"遍"、"次"、"下"、"阵"均为动量词。"遍"表示一个(套)动作从开始到结束的整个过程,如"再讲一遍这个故事"。"次"表示行为或动作的次数,一般用于能反复出现的事情,如"去了三次"。"下"表示动作的次数,一般用于短时间的动作。"一下"还有缓和语气的作用。"阵"表示可持续的动作,如"一阵猛打"。根据题义,这里的"去"应该是一个反复出现的事情,选 B。

**113.** 请把课文再读一_____。

  A. 趟        B. 回

  C. 遍        D. 阵

**题解**：正确答案是 C。"趟"一般指来回行走的次数。"回"表示动作的次数，也用于(能)反复出现的动作，比"次"的口语色彩更浓。"阵"表示可持续的动作，如"一阵猛打"。"遍"表示一个(套)动作从开始到结束的整个过程，如"再讲一遍这个故事"。根据题义选 C。

**114.** 他拿起苹果咬了一大_____。

  A. 遍        B. 回

  C. 次        D. 口

**题解**：正确答案是 D。"口"作为临时动量词，可用于表示口腔动作次数。用法有二：(1)动+数+口，例如："被蛇咬了一口。"(2)数+口+动，例如："一口吞下。"此处属于用法(1)。"一大"只能修饰来自于身体部位的临时量词，如"踢一大脚"、"打一大嘴巴"。因此此题的正确答案是 D。

**115.** 他不小心撞了她一_____。

  A. 次        B. 下

  C. 遍        D. 趟

**题解**：正确答案是 B。"遍"、"次"、"下"、"趟"均为动量词。"遍"表示一个(套)动作从开始到结束的整个过程，如"再讲一遍这个故事"。"次"表示行为或动作的次数，一般用于能反复出现的事情，如"去了三次"。"下"表示动作的次数，一般用于短时间的动作。"一下"还有缓和语气的作用。"趟"表示来回走动的次数，如"去一趟银行"。根据题义，"不小心撞了她"不会是一套动作，也不会是反复出现的动作，只能是一个持续时间短暂的动作，所以选 B。"一下"在这里有缓和语气的作用。

### 否定副词

**116.** 昨夜他_____睡着觉。

  A. 不        B. 没

  C. 别        D. 甭

**题解**：正确答案是 B。"不"、"没(有)"、"别"、"甭"都是否定副词，都可以放在动词或形容词前，对动作或者性状作否定的说明，但用法不同。在修饰动词的时候，"不"是对判断或意愿进行否定，否定的对象与时间特征无关，可以是现在、将来，也可以是过去。"没(有)"是对已然的行为或动作进行否定，所否定的对象一定是已经发生的事情。"别"和"甭"表示劝阻或禁止。根据题意，此处是对已然的行为进行否定，故选 B。

117. 你走吧,她_____想见你。

　　A. 不　　　　　　　　　　B. 没
　　C. 没有　　　　　　　　　D. 别

**题解**:正确答案是 A。"不"、"没"、"没有"、"别"都是否定副词,都可以放在动词或形容词前,对动作或者性状进行否定,但它们的用法不同。在修饰动词的时候,"不"是对判断或意愿进行否定,否定的对象与时间特征无关,可以是现在、将来,也可以是过去。"没(有)"是对已然的行为或动作进行否定,所否定的对象一定是已经发生的事情。"别"表示劝阻或禁止。根据题意,此处是对未然的意愿进行否定,故选 A。

118. 你_____做白日梦了。

　　A. 不　　　　　　　　　　B. 没
　　C. 别　　　　　　　　　　D. 没有

**题解**:正确答案是 C。"不"、"没"、"没有"、"别"都是否定副词,都可以放在动词或形容词前,对动作或者性状进行否定,但它们的用法不同。在修饰动词的时候,"不"是对判断或意愿进行否定,否定的对象与时间特征无关,可以是现在、将来,也可以是过去。"没(有)"是对已然的行为或动作进行否定,所否定的对象一定是已经发生的事情。"别"表示劝阻或禁止。根据题意,此处是表示劝阻的语气,故选 C。

119. 我的英语_____。

　　A. 不说得好　　　　　　　B. 没说得好
　　C. 说得不好　　　　　　　D. 说得没好

**题解**:正确答案是 C。"英语说得好不好"是一种评价,对动作进行描写、评价、判断在汉语中一般由"得"加上形容词短语或形容词来表达,如果这个描写、评价或判断是否定性的,否定词语一定要放在"得"后,形容词或形容词短语之前。对一种性状进行否定性评价应该用"不",所以此题选 C。

120. 下了火车,他_____旅店。

　　A. 立刻不去　　　　　　　B. 立刻没去
　　C. 没立刻去　　　　　　　D. 立刻别去

**题解**:正确答案是 C。"不"、"没"、"没有"、"别"都是否定副词,都可以放在动词或形容词前,对动作或者性状进行否定,但它们的用法不同。在修饰动词的时候,"不"是对判断或意愿进行否定,否定的对象与时间特征无关,可以是现在、将来,也可以是过去。"没(有)"是对已然的行为或动作进行否定,所否定的对象一定是已经发生的事情。"别"表示劝阻或禁止。根据句义,这是个表示已然判断的句子,这里应当是否定"去"这个动作已然发生的事件,故排除 A。这不是一个表示劝阻或禁止的句子,所以也可以排除 D。当"没"与其它副词连用时,"没"

只能放在其他副词的前边,故选C。

**121.** 明天上午我＿＿＿＿＿去上课。
    A. 没                    B. 没有
    C. 别                    D. 不

**题解:**正确答案是D。"不"、"没"、"没有"、"别"都是否定副词,都可以放在动词或形容词前,对动作或者性状进行否定,但它们的用法不同。在修饰动词的时候,"不"是对判断或意愿进行否定,否定的对象与时间特征无关,可以是现在、将来,也可以是过去。"没(有)"是对已然的行为或动作进行否定,所否定的对象一定是已经发生的事情。"别"表示劝阻或禁止。这里说的是"明天上午"将要发生的事,所以可以排除A"没"和B"没有";这里说的是"我"自己的事,也不是对别人进行劝阻,因此还可以排除C"别"。最后只有D"不"是惟一的选择了,它否定的是意愿。

**122.** 那条裙子漂亮,这条＿＿＿＿＿漂亮。
    A. 不                    B. 没
    C. 没有                  D. 别

**题解:**正确答案是A。"不"、"没"、"没有"、"别"都是否定副词,都可以放在动词或形容词前,对动作或者性状进行否定,但它们的用法不同。在修饰形容词的时候,"不"是对性质进行否定,"没(有)"是对已然的行为或动作进行否定,它修饰形容词时,那个形容词必须是表示变化的动态词语,不能是表示性质的静态词语。"别"表示劝阻或禁止。"漂亮"是一种静态的性质,只能用"不"否定。

**123.** 我＿＿＿＿＿看那个片子了。
    A. 没有                  B. 没
    C. 不是                  D. 不

**题解:**正确答案是D。"不"、"没"、"没有"都是否定副词,都可以放在动词或形容词前,对动作或者性状进行否定,但它们的用法不同。在修饰动词的时候,"不"是对判断或意愿进行否定,否定的对象与时间特征无关,可以是现在、将来,也可以是过去。"没(有)"是对已然的行为或动作进行否定,所否定的对象一定是已经发生的事情。根据句义,这个句子表达的是一种意愿,所以应该由"不"来否定,故选D。另外,否定副词"没有"与句末语气词"了"共现是有条件的,即前面应该有"好久"、"三个星期"等表示有限时段的词语。这个句子没有表示有限时段的词语,所以应该排除A、B。

**124.** 快＿＿＿＿＿吵了,老师来了!
    A. 不                    B. 别
    C. 没                    D. 没有

**题解:**正确答案是B。"不"、"没"、"没有"、"别"都是否定副词,都可以放在动词或形容词前,对动作或者性状进行否定,但它们的用法不同。在修饰动词的时候,"不"是对判断或意愿进行否定,否定的对象与时间特征无关,可以是现在、将来,也可以是过去。"没(有)"是对已然的行为或动作进行否定,所否定的对象一定是已经发生的事情。"别"表示劝阻或禁止。这个句子显然是表示劝阻的意思,所以选"别"。

125. 时间_____早了,大家收拾一下起程吧。

  A. 不         B. 别

  C. 没         D. 没有

**题解**:正确答案是 A。"不"、"没"、"没有"、"别"都是否定副词,都可以放在动词或形容词前,对动作或者性状进行否定,但它们的用法不同。在修饰动词的时候,"不"是对判断或意愿进行否定,否定的对象与时间特征无关,可以是现在、将来,也可以是过去。"没(有)"是对已然的行为或动作进行否定,所否定的对象一定是已经发生的事情。"别"表示劝阻或禁止。"早"是一种性质,应该用"不"来否定。另外,否定副词"没有"与句末语气词"了"共现是有条件的,即前面应该有"好久"、"三个星期"等表示有限时段的词语。这个句子没有这个条件,所以应该排除"没"和"没有"。这个句子的第一个分句也不是表示劝阻,所以也不能用"别"。

### 时间副词

126. 前天晚上十点多_____家。

  A. 才我回到       B. 我回才到

  C. 我才回到       D. 我回到才

**题解**:正确答案是 C。"才"是一个时间副词,表说话者认为动作实现得晚或慢。如果不是疑问句,此时它的前面一定有表示时间的词语,如"我上午十点才起床"、"他们用了两年时间才到达那里";"才"的位置应该放于主语后,动词前,故选 C。

127. 刚吃过午饭,_____朋友了。

  A. 他就去看       B. 就他去看

  C. 去看他就       D. 他去看就

**题解**:正确答案是 A。"就"作为时间副词,用来表示两个紧接着发生的动作或事件的后一个动作或事件,"就"应该放在动词前,主语后。所以选 A。

128. 世界公园很远,我们走了两个小时_____到。

  A. 就         B. 总

  C. 才         D. 常

**题解**:正确答案是 C。"就"和"才"都是时间副词,它们表达的是与具体时间相关的行为动作或事件,因此句子中都有表示时段的词语,如"两小时、三天、十年";"总"和"常"也可以表示时间,但是它们所表达的是惯常性的行为动作或事件。这个句子谈论的是一个与具体时间相关的事件,所以应该排除 B、D。"才"表达的意思是说话者认为动作行为实现得晚或慢,"就"恰好相反,它表达的是说话人认为动作或行为实现得早或快。这个句子中的"两个小时"在说话人的主观想法里是时间长,所以应该选"才"。

129. 听你这么一说,我_____知道他是老师。

　　A. 就才　　　　　　　　　　B. 才
　　C. 常常　　　　　　　　　　D. 正在

题解:正确答案是 B。"才"在这里是关联副词,用于复句的后一分句,表示只有在某种条件下,或由于某种原因,然后怎么样。前一分句常有"只有、必须、要;因为,由于;为了"等关联词语与之呼应。"常常"是一个频率副词,"正在"是一个时间副词,表动作在进行中或状态在持续中。根据题意,此处应选关联副词"才"。"就"和"才"语义相对,不能连用,故排除 A。

130. 以前_____百货大楼买东西。

　　A. 曾经我去　　　　　　　　B. 已经我去
　　C. 我经常去　　　　　　　　D. 刚我去

题解:正确答案是 C。"曾经"、"已经"、"经常"、"刚"都是与时间有关的副词。"曾经"表示从前有过某种行为或情况,常常和"过"配合使用,如"我曾经当过老师";"已经"表示行为动作或事件已然完成,而且完成时间就在不久以前,其结果对当前情况有影响;"经常"是一频度副词,表示行为、动作发生的次数多,可以是过去某一段时间某种行为、动作发生的次数多,也可以是惯常情况,从过去一直持续到当前;"刚"表示和说话时间非常近的过去发生了某件事。它们都必须放于动词前做状语,所以只有 C 符合条件。

131. 他_____旷课三天了。

　　A. 常常　　　　　　　　　　B. 已经
　　C. 正在　　　　　　　　　　D. 曾经

题解:正确答案是 B。"常常"、"已经"、"正在"、"曾经"都是与时间有关的副词。"常常"是一频度副词,表示行为、动作发生的次数多,可以是过去某一段时间某种行为、动作发生的次数多,也可以是惯常情况,从过去一直持续到当前;"已经"表示行为动作或事件已然完成,而且完成时间就在不久以前,其结果对当前情况有影响;"正在"表动作在进行中或状态在持续中。句末语气词"了"在这个句子中表达一种结果意义,与表示已然完成意义的"已经"语义相配,所以选 B。

### 范围副词

**132.** 今晚_____看电影。

  A. 都我们大家     B. 都我们大家

  C. 我们都大家     D. 我们大家都

**题解：** 正确答案是 D。"都"作为范围副词，表示总括全部，除问话以外，所总括的对象必须放在"都"前，这样就可以排除 A、B；在句法上"都"修饰它后面的动词或形容词，表示"都"所限定的事物没有例外地发生或具有谓语动词所表达的行为动作或形容词所表达的性状。这里总括的对象是"我们大家"，动词是"看"，只有 D 符合条件。

**133.** 大家_____生日快乐。

  A. 向她都祝贺     B. 都祝贺向她

  C. 都向她祝贺     D. 祝贺都向她

**题解：** 正确答案是 C。"都"和"向她"在这个句子里都是状语，应该放在动词"祝贺"前，因此可以排除 B 和 D；"都"和介词结构同时做状语的时候，因为"都"不能和它所总括的成分分离，所以总是介词结构里动词最近，因此 A 是错的。

**134.** 我_____帮助你，没别的目的。

  A. 想只        B. 只想

  C. 都想        D. 想都

**题解：** 正确答案是 B。"只"和"都"都是范围副词，"只"表示有限范围，"都"表示周遍范围，"只"所限定的对象在它后边，如"只有一个孩子"，而"都"所总括的对象在它前边，而且总括的对象不能是一个单数名词，如"他们都来了"；"我"是一个单数，不能用"都"总括，可排除 C、D。副词在句法上修饰它后面的动词，根据题义，"只"在这里修饰"想帮助你"，因此选 B。

**135.** _____两千个座位。

  A. 一共有这个礼堂    B. 这个礼堂有一共

  C. 这个礼堂一共有    D. 有一共这个礼堂

**题解：** 正确答案是 C。"一共"也是一个范围副词，放在动词前做状语，后边总有数量词做动词的宾语。在这个句子中，只有 C"一共"在动词前，所以选 C。

### 程度副词

**136.** 今天的天气很冷，还_____。

  A. 很下大雪      B. 很大下雪

  C. 下雪很大      D. 下了很大的雪

**题解：** 正确答案是 D。"很"作为程度副词，用在形容词前，所以排除 A。"很+形容词"不能放在动词或动词结构前做状语,所以排除 B。"很 + 形容词"可以做谓语,说明一个体词性话题,"下雪"是谓词性的,前面又加上一个修饰性的"还",不能充任"很大"的话题,所以排除 C。"很 + 形容词 + 的"可以修饰名词,故选 D。

137. 你_____不懂事了,怎么能抢占爷爷的座位呢?
   A. 太  B. 很
   C. 非常  D. 十分

题解:正确答案是 A。"太"、"很"、"非常"、"十分"都是程度副词,但是它们在所表达的程度上和具体用法上是有区别的。"太 +(不)+ 形 + 了"是一种固定搭配。

138. 这个电影_____。
   A. 多么很好看  B. 很多么好看
   C. 很好看  D. 好看多么

题解:正确答案是 C。从意义上说,"多么"是程度副词,表示程度很高。有夸张语气和强烈的感情色彩,多用于感叹句中(1)多么 + 形/动(啊),如"多么漂亮啊、多么懂事啊、多么会说话呀"(2)多么 + 不 + 形/动(啊),如"多么不懂事呀、多么不会说话呀",句末常带"啊(呀、哪、哇)"。"很"也是程度副词,但是它所表达的程度不如"多么"深。从搭配上看,两个程度副词不能同时用来修饰限制一个形容词,所以 A、B 可以排除。"多么"在句法位置上只能放在动词或谓词结构前面做状语,所以 D 也可以排除。只有 C 是正确的。

139. 她长得_____!
   A. 非常漂亮极了  B. 很漂亮极了
   C. 十分漂亮极了  D. 非常漂亮

题解:正确答案是 D。"非常"是程度副词,表示程度很高。"极"也是程度副词,但是它们的用法不同。"非常"和"极"都可以做状语,而"极 + 了"经常做补语,"非常"没有这种用法。两个程度副词不能同时用来修饰限制一个形容词,所以 A、B、C 都可以排除。

140. 操场上的人_____?
   A. 很多不很多  B. 很多不多
   C. 很多吗  D. 多不很多

题解:正确答案是 C。这是一个疑问句的形式,"程度副词 + 形容词"做谓语的疑问形式只有特指问形式,没有选择问和正反问形式,所以 A、B、D 都是错的,应选 C。

141. 她的歌声_____美呀!
   A. 多  B. 很
   C. 更  D. 太

题解:正确答案是 A。"多"、"很"、"更"、"太"都是程度副词,但是它们所表达的程度和用法有所不同。"多"有夸张语气和强烈的感情色彩,多用于感叹句中,构成"多+(不)形容词"格式,句末常带"啊(呀、哪、哇)。"等语气词与之呼应,"很"和"更"没有这种用法。"太"也有夸张语气和强烈的感情色彩,但是在感叹句中,与"太+(不)形容词"格式相呼应的感叹词是"啦"。这个句子的句末语气词是"呀",故选 A。

### 关联副词

142. 这事刚说完,怎么＿＿＿＿＿＿提起来了?
  A. 再  B. 又
  C. 还  D. 也

**题解:**正确答案是 B。"再"、"又"、"还"、"也"都是可以表达动作行为的重复、反复或继续的关联副词。在表示动作重复或继续时,"再"、"还"均表示未实现的动作,"又"表示已实现的动作。"也"和"又"的区别是,"也"表示类同,表示与某一行为动作或性状同类性质的行为动作或性状在不同的对象身上出现了,所以用"也"的时候应该有一个可比项。"又"表示重复、反复,通常表示同一性质的行为动作在相同的对象身上出现了。根据题义,"刚说完"和"提起"属于同一性质的行为动作,因此选"又",此处"又"表示动作行为重复或反复,兼有责备或不满的语气。

143. 这首歌真好听,我想＿＿＿＿＿＿听一遍。
  A. 再  B. 又
  C. 还  D. 也

**题解:**正确答案是 A。"再"、"又"、"还"、"也"都是可以表达动作行为的重复、反复或继续的关联副词。在表示动作重复或继续时,"再"、"还"均表示未实现的动作,"又"表示已实现的动作。"想"是表打算的能愿动词,因为"听"是一个未实现的动作,排除 B。"也"和"又"的区别是,"也"表示类同,可以是已然的,也可以是未然的,表示与某一行为动作或性状同类性质的行为动作或性状在不同的对象身上将出现或已出现,所以用"也"的时候应该有一个可比项,"又"一定是未然的,也没有可比项。"再"与"还"的区别是:"还"应放于能愿动词前,"再"放在主要动词前。根据题意和句子的结构,应选 A。

144. 你说他不是好人,其实你＿＿＿＿＿＿不怎么样。
  A. 再  B. 又
  C. 还  D. 也

**题解:**正确答案是 D。"再"、"又"、"还"、"也"都是可以表达动作行为的重复、反复或继续的关联副词。在表示动作重复或继续时,"再"、"还"均表示未实现的动作,"又"表示已实现的动作。"也"和"又"的区别是,"也"表示类同,表示与某一行为动作或性状同类性质的行为动作或性状在不同的对象身上出现或将出现,所以用"也"的时候一定有一个可比项。"又"表示重复、反复,通常表示同一性质的行为动作在相同的对象身上出现了。这个句子"他"是"你"的可比项,关联成分前后的两部分性质相类,所以选"也"做关联词。

145. 我说过我不爱他,可他＿＿＿＿＿是纠缠不休。

    A. 再　　　　　　　　　　　　B. 又
    C. 还　　　　　　　　　　　　D. 也

**题解**:正确答案是 C。"再"、"又"、"还"、"也"都是可以表达动作行为的重复、反复或继续的关联副词。在表示动作重复或继续时,"再"、"还"均表示未实现的动作,"又"表示已实现的动作。"也"和"又"的区别是,"也"表示类同,表示与某一行为动作或性状同类性质的行为动作或性状在不同的对象身上出现或将出现,所以用"也"的时候一定有一个可比项。"又"表示重复、反复,通常表示同一性质的行为动作在相同的对象身上出现了。另外,"还"还有一个用法,就是表示动作行为的继续进行或状况的继续存在,含有"仍旧"、"依然"的意思。其他三个关联副词都没有这种用法,所以根据句义,本句选 C。

## 介词

146. 我打算今天下午＿＿＿＿＿。

    A. 跟我同学一起去图书馆　　　　B. 一起去图书馆跟我同学
    C. 图书馆一起去跟我同学　　　　D. 跟我同学去图书馆一起

**题解**:正确答案是 A。"跟"是介词,与后边的名词性成分构成介词结构做状语,位置是在动词性结构前,所以 B、C 应该排除。"一起"是副词,在句子中也做状语,也应该放在动词性成分之前,因此 D 也应该排除。

147. 你是＿＿＿＿＿?

    A. 什么地方来的从　　　　　　　B. 来的从什么地方
    C. 从什么地方来的　　　　　　　D. 什么地方从来的

**题解**:正确答案是 C。"从"是介词,与后边的名词性成分构成介词结构做状语,所以 A 和 D 都是错的。介词结构的位置是在动词性结构前,所以 B 也应该排除。这样只有 C 是正确的。

148. 小王＿＿＿＿＿朋友那儿直接去了书店。

    A. 当　　　　　　　　　　　　　B. 在
    C. 离　　　　　　　　　　　　　D. 从

**题解**:正确答案是 D。"当"、"在"、"离"、"从"都是介词,其中"在"、"离"、"从"都可以与表示空间位置或时间内容有关的名词性成分结合起来表达空间方位、空间范围、时点或时段。"当"表示时间,后边的名词性成分应该是表示时点的,如

"当我看见他的时候,他正在买车票"。"朋友那儿"是表示空间位置的词语,所以可以排除"当"。"在"表示空间位置的位置点或空间范围,如"在车站、在操场"。"离"表达两点之间的距离,如"天津离北京比较近"。"从"可表示空间段的起点或时间段的起点,当表示空间段的起点时,后面一般要跟表处所或方位的词语。根据句义选"从"。

149. 他每天_____。

  A. 从家去学校七点钟　　　　B. 去学校从家七点钟
  C. 七点钟从家去学校　　　　D. 从家七点钟去学校

**题解**:正确答案是 C。解释Ⅰ:一个句子如果有不止一个状语,汉语状语的排列顺序是:(1)表示时间的状语;(2)表示语气、关联句子的状语;(3)描写动作者的状语;(4)表示目的、依据、关涉、协同的状语;(5)表示处所、空间、方向、路线的状语;(6)表示对象的状语;(7)描写动作的状语。"七点钟"是时间状语,"从家"是处所和方向状语,因此应该时间状语在前,所以应选 C。解释Ⅱ:时间词语是名词性的,在句子中可充当主语或宾语,而介词结构只能充当状语或补语,由"从"构成的介词结构只能做状语,主语的位置在句首,状语的位置在动词前,因此"他每天七点钟从家去学校"实际上有三重主语:"他"、"每天"、"七点钟",这是这个句子的三重话题。

150. 他_____花园里散步。

  A. 从　　　　　　　　　　　B. 在
  C. 往　　　　　　　　　　　D. 向

**题解**:正确答案是 B。"从"与表示处所或时间的名词结合表示行为动作发生的起点或时间的起点,这时后边要有"到"、"去"、"向"、"朝"、"往"等表示方向的词语与之呼应,有时也能与处所名词结合表达通过的处所,这时动词通常是"经过"、"路过"等。这个句子不符合这些条件,所以可以排除 A。"在"表示动作发生或事物存在的处所。"往"、"向"表示行为动作的方向。"散步"是一个没有方向的动词,因此不能与表示方向的"往"、"向"结合,所以也可以排除 C、D。

151. 他_____我挥挥手就走了。

  A. 向　　　　　　　　　　　B. 从
  C. 往　　　　　　　　　　　D. 在

**题解**:正确答案是 A。"向"、"往"都可以表示行为动作的方向。但是"向"后边的名词性成分可以是一个对象,也可以是一个具有空间方位特征的名词性成分,而"往"后边的名词性成分不能是一个对象,只能是一个具有空间方位特征的名词性成分,"我"不具有空间方位特征,所以只能选"向"。"从"与表示处所或时间的名词结合表示行为动作发生的起点或时间的起点,这时后边要有"到"、"去"、"向"、"朝"、"往"等表示方向的词语与之呼应,有时也能与处所名词结合表达通过的处所,这时动词通常是"经过"、"路过"等。这个句子不符合这些条件,所以可以排除 B。"在"表示动作发生或事物存在的处所,后边连接的应该是表达空间方位的名词性成分。"我"不是表达空间方位的,故排除 D。

152. 我喜欢住窗户_____阳的房间。
  A. 往         B. 在
  C. 朝         D. 从

**题解**:正确答案是 C。"往"、"在"、"朝"、"从"都是与空间方位有关系的介词,"往"、"朝"具有方向性,"在"、"从"没有。"朝"表示面对的方向,"往"表示行为动作的方向,后边的名词性成分只能是一个具有空间方位特征的名词性成分,"从"与表示处所或时间的名词结合,表示行为动作发生的起点或时间的起点,这时后边要有"到"、"去"、"向"、"朝"、"往"等表示方向的词语与之呼应,有时也能与处所名词结合表达通过的处所,这时动词通常是"经过"、"路过"等。"阳"是面对的方向,所以选"朝"。

153. 他家_____学校只有两公里。
  A. 从         B. 向
  C. 往         D. 离

**题解**:正确答案是 D。"从"与表示处所或时间的名词结合表示行为动作发生的起点或时间的起点,这时后边要有"到"、"去"、"向"、"朝"、"往"等表示方向的词语与之呼应,有时也能与处所名词结合表达通过的处所,这时动词通常是"经过"、"路过"等。"向"、"往"都可以表示行为动作的方向。但是"向"后边的名词性成分可以是一个对象,也可以是一个具有空间方位特征的名词性成分,而"往"后边的名词性成分不能是一个对象,只能是一个具有空间方位特征的名词性成分。"离"表示两点之间的距离(空间或时间),后边应该有表示距离的数量词语,这个句子正好符合这个要求,所以选 D。

154. 老张_____早上一直等到晚上。
  A. 从         B. 在
  C. 离         D. 当

**答案**:正确答案是 A。"从"与表示处所或时间的名词结合表示行为动作发生的起点或时间的起点,这时后边要有"到"、"去"、"向"、"朝"、"往"等表示方向的词语与之呼应,这个句子正好具备时间词语和"到"这两个条件,所以选"从"。"离"表示两点之间的距离(空间或时间),后边应该有表示距离的数量词语。"在"表示动作发生或事物存在的处所,后边连接的应该是表达空间方位的名词性成分。"当"表示时点。所以 B、C、D 都不合适。

155. _____太阳升起的时候,草原上就会响起悠扬的牧歌。
  A. 当         B. 朝
  C. 离         D. 向

**题解**:正确答案是 A。"当"后边应该是表示时间的词语,"太阳升起的时候"恰好是表示时间的词语,所以选择 A。"朝"后边应该接续表示方向的词语,例如"朝南"、"朝北"、"朝太阳升起的地方";"向"后边也应该接续表示方向的词语,例如"向南"、"向北"、"向太阳升起的地方";"离"后边应该接续表示处所的词语,而且还要有表示距离的数量词语或者"远"、"近"这样的形容词。

156. 李先生_____很热情。

  A. 不对他          B. 对他不

  C. 对不他          D. 他对不

题解:正确答案是 B。"对"作为介词,后边可引进行为动作的对象或关系者,例如"他",这样只有 A、B 符合条件。在"对 + NP + VP"组合中,如果 VP 是动词或者动词词组,否定词"不"应该放在"对"前,例如"不对他负责"、"不对他发脾气";如果 VP 是形容词或者形容词词组,"不"应该放在形容词或形容词组的前面,例如"对他不好"、"对我不怎么热情",因此应选 B。

157. 我们要_____这件事进行调查。

  A. 对于          B. 关于

  C. 对           D. 有关

题解:正确答案是 C。"对于"、"关于"、"对"这三个介词都可以在后边引出动作的对象或相关事物,但是"对于"和"关于"只能用在句子的开头部分,不能用在句子的中间,例如我们可以说"对于这件事我们要进行调查",或者"关于这件事我们要进行调查",而不能说"我们要对于/关于这件事进行调查"。介词"对"构成介词结构以后既可以放在句子开头的部分,也可以放在句子的中间,例如本题可以说:"我们要对这件事进行调查"、"我们对这件事要进行调查"或"对这件事我们要进行调查"。"有关"是动词,一般要与介词"与"连用,构成"与……有关"结构,如"空气不好与汽车尾气有关"。

158. 张教授明天下午_____。

  A. 为我们作报告       B. 作报告为我们

  C. 作为我们报告       D. 报告作为我们

题解:正确答案是 A。"为"是介词,与后边的名词性词语结合以后构成介词结构,这个介词结构只能放在谓词性词语的前面做状语,在这个句子里,"作报告"是谓词性词语,只有 A"为我们"在谓词性词语的前面,所以选 A。

159. 上飞机前_____。

  A. 她给买了我一个小礼物     B. 她买了我给一个小礼物

  C. 她给我买了一个小礼物     D. 她买给了一个小礼物我

题解:正确答案是 C。"给"是介词,它与后边的名词性词语结合后构成介词结构做状语,出现的位置是谓词性词语之前,例如"给我买礼物";或者构成介词结构以后做补语,出现的位置是谓词性词语之后,例如"扔给我一件衣服";还可以用在被动句中,作为被动态的标记,例如"把自己给锁在外边了"。"给"还可以是动词,出现在双宾语结构中,例如"给我一件礼物";或者出现在连谓结构中,例如"买一件礼物给我"。本题中的"给"是介词,只有 C 符合介词结构做状语的条件。

160. 她_____去了。

  A. 一起跟新郎度蜜月　　　　　　B. 一起度蜜月跟新郎
  C. 度蜜月跟新郎一起　　　　　　D. 跟新郎一起度蜜月

题解:正确答案是 D。"跟"是介词,与后边的名词性成分构成介词结构做状语,出现的位置是谓词性词语之前。由"跟"构成的介词结构不能做补语,所以不能出现在谓词性结构的后边,这样就排除了 B 和 C。如果有不只一个状语,介词结构应该排在前面,所以我们选择"跟新郎一起度蜜月",排除"一起跟新郎度蜜月"。

161. 他_____。

  A. 高比他姐姐　　　　　　　　　B. 比高他姐姐
  C. 比他姐姐高　　　　　　　　　D. 高他姐姐比

题解:正确答案是 C。"比"字句出现在这样的结构里:$NP_1$ + 比 + $NP_2$ + VP,由"比"把两个比较项连接起来。作为谓语的 VP 可以是形容词、形容词短语、动词短语。如:"这座山比那座山高"、"这座山比那座上高多了"、"他比我更有资格当总理"。由"比"构成的介词结构不能做补语,所以"比 $NP_2$"不能出现在谓词性词语的后面,这样就排除了 A;"比"字不能单独放在谓词性成分前做成分,也不能单独放在句末做成分,这样也排除了 B 和 D。故选 C。

162. 我努力学习是准备_____祖国贡献力量。

  A. 为　　　　　　　　　　　　　B. 为了
  C. 因为　　　　　　　　　　　　D. 作为

题解:正确答案是 A。"为"作为介词,可引进动作的受益者。"为了"是连词,表示目的,后面应该接续的是表示目的的从句;"因为"也是连词,表示原因,后面接续的应该是一个表示原因的从句。"祖国贡献力量"不能单独成句,所以它不是一个从句,这样就排除了 B 和 C。"作为"是动词,后边只能接续名词性成分,也可排除。

163. 我_____。

  A. 没把这几个字写在纸上　　　　B. 把这几个字没写在纸上
  C. 没把这几个字在纸上写　　　　D. 把这几个字写没在纸上

题解:正确答案是 A。在"把"字句里,否定副词应该放在"把"字之前,因此排除了 B 和 D。在"把"字句里,如果"把"后边的谓词性成分不是由"一 + V"构成的,应该在动词后面有补充性成分,例如补语或者是体貌标记"了",否则句子在结构上不能被接受,这样也排除了 C。

**164.** 他的数学作业＿＿＿＿＿＿。

　　A．叫他做完了　　　　　　　　B．做让他完了

　　C．做完了　　　　　　　　　　D．被他做完了

**题解**：正确答案是 C。汉语的被动句可以由"被"、"叫"、"让"构成,但是被动句的成句是有条件的。在"X 被 Y + VP"这样的被动结构中,只有当 X 在语义上对于 Y 来说是典型的受事(patient)时,结构才能成立。例如"他的作业本被他弄丢了","他的作业本"对于"弄丢了"来说是典型的受事,"他的数学作业被他作得一塌糊涂"中"他的数学作业"对于"作得一塌糊涂"来说也是典型的受事。如果位于 X 位置上的成分只是个普通的话题,在汉语里不需要用被动句来表达。所以我们选择 C。

**165.** 这个照相机＿＿＿＿＿＿。

　　A．叫弄坏了　　　　　　　　　B．让弄坏了

　　C．把弄坏了　　　　　　　　　D．被弄坏了

**题解**：正确答案是 D。现代汉语的被动句可以用"被"、"叫"、"让"、"给"做标记。但使用"叫/让"的时候,施事一定要出现,例如"照相机叫孩子弄坏了","照相机让孩子弄坏了",使用"被"的时候不受这个限制,施事者可以出现,也可以不出现。"把"是表示致使意义的介词,出现在被动句中只能与"给"一起用,如"孩子把照相机给弄坏了"。

### 连词

**166.** 你今天晚上去看电影＿＿＿＿＿＿听音乐会?

　　A．或者　　　　　　　　　　　B．还是

　　C．跟　　　　　　　　　　　　D．和

**题解**：正确答案是 B。"或者"和"还是"都是表示选择关系的连词,但二者也有重要区别。"或者"是提出两个(或两个以上的)可能性或对象供选择,意在所选定的必居其一,不能用于疑问句。"还是"是指出两个(或者两个以上的)可能性或对象,意在询问选择其中的哪一项,只用于疑问句。应当指出,用"还是"的句子如果成为一个更大的句子的包孕成分时不表示疑问,例如:(1)用"还是"的小句做前边动词的宾语,例如"我真的不知道你是中国人还是日本人"。(2)含有"还是"的小句做前分句,后边有总括性、评价性的后续分句,例如:"他今天晚上去看电影还是听音乐会,我不知道。""和"、"跟"连接两个体词性成分,不表示选择关系,所以排除。

**167.** 他正是＿＿＿＿＿＿身体不好,才天天坚持练长跑。

　　A．为了　　　　　　　　　　　B．虽然

　　C．因为　　　　　　　　　　　D．原因

**题解：** 正确答案是 C。"为了"是连接目的从句的连词，"虽然"是连接转折从句的连词，"因为"是连接原因从句的连词，根据题意，这是一个表示因果关系的复句，这里需用一个表因果关系的连词，故选 C。"原因"是名词，应该排除。

168．请把这封信交给小张＿＿＿＿＿＿小王。

  A．还是         B．并且

  C．或者         D．而且

**题解：** 正确答案是 C。"还是"、"或者"都是表示选择关系的连词，但二者也有重要区别。"或者"是提出两个（或两个以上的）可能性或对象供选择，意在所选定的必居其一，不能用于疑问句。"还是"是指出两个（或者两个以上的）可能性或对象，意在询问选择其中的哪一项，只用于疑问句。应当指出，用"还是"的句子如果成为一个更大的句子的包孕成分时不表示疑问，例如："我真的不知道你是中国人还是日本人"。"他今天晚上去看电影还是听音乐会，我不知道。"这是一个叙述句，而且不是一个包孕句，所以我们排除"还是"。"并且、而且"连接两个谓词性成分，表示除所说的意思之外，还有更进一层的意思。这里的"小张"、"小王"都是体词性的成分，所以排除 B、D。

169．他家的花园很大＿＿＿＿＿＿很漂亮。

  A．而且         B．和

  C．跟          D．虽然

**题解：** 正确答案是 A。"和"、"跟"都是表示并列关系的连词，它们连接的两个部分是体词性的，"很大"和"很漂亮"都是谓词性的。所以排除 B、C。"虽然"是表转折关系的连词，它和"但是"合起来用，所连接的两个谓词性成分语义相反或者相对，也可以排除。"而且"连接两个谓词性成分，表示意思更进一层，是表递进关系的连词，故选 A。

### 助词

170．上星期天我们去＿＿＿＿＿＿几个公园。

  A．的         B．得

  C．了         D．着

**题解：** 正确答案是 C。"的"出现在动词后边可以表示动态，但是句子的话题部分必须是说话人要强调的对象，例如"是我去的上海"，用"是"强调话题"我"，又比如"我上星期天去的上海"，用重音强调话题"上星期天"，又如"我坐飞机去的上海"用重音强调"坐飞机"。根据题意，这里没有强调的意思，排除"的"。"得"是结构助词，用在动词后，它后边的成分是表示结果或者可能的补语，应该是谓词性的，这里的"几个公园"是体词性的，应该是动词的宾语，也排除"得"。"着"、"了"都是动态助词，"了"表示动作实现，"着"表持续态。根据题意，"去"是上星期天完成的动作,故选 C。

**171.** 我没有看＿＿＿＿＿这本小说。

　　A．了　　　　　　　　　　　B．着
　　C．过　　　　　　　　　　　D．得

**题解：**正确答案是 C。"了"是表示实现体的动态助词,不能和"没有"共现(co-occurrence),也就是说不能出现"没有……了"这样的句子。"着"是表示持续态的动态助词,也不能和"没有"共现。"过"是表示经历态的动态助词,表示过去曾经有的事情,否定式是"没(有)＋动＋过"。"得"是结构助词,用在动词后,它后边的成分是表示结果或者可能的补语,应该是谓词性的。

**172.** 现在我们的生活水平提高＿＿＿＿＿。

　　A．着　　　　　　　　　　　B．过
　　C．呢　　　　　　　　　　　D．了

**题解：**正确答案是 D。"着"、"过"分别表示持续体和经历体,"呢"用在叙述句的末尾,表示动作持续或者进行的状态,常和"正、正在、在(哪里)"或"着"等相搭配。"了"可作为动态助词兼语气词,放在句末,表示情况发生了变化。"生活水平提高"是表示变化的,因此选"了"。

**173.** 上星期他＿＿＿＿＿。

　　A．旷过课三次　　　　　　　　B．旷三次课过
　　C．旷过三次课　　　　　　　　D．三次旷课过

**题解：**正确答案是 C。"过"总是在动词后,宾语前。只有 A、C 符合条件;这里"三次"是数量词做宾语"课"的定语,应该放在名词"课"前,所以 A 也是不对的。

**174.** 经过一个月的努力,他已经有＿＿＿＿＿不少进步。

　　A．过　　　　　　　　　　　B．了
　　C．着　　　　　　　　　　　D．的

**题解：**正确答案是 B。"过"、"了"、"着"、"的"都是体标记(aspect markers),其中"过"表示"有过经历","了"表示"实现某种变化","着"表示"某种动作行为正在进行或持续","的"表示"对某一动作行为以及与该动作行为有关的论元的肯定",通常可以变成"是……的……"结构,"是"后边的成分就是肯定的内容。"已经有不少进步"在意义上应该属于"实现某种变化",所以选择"了"。

**175.** 气温降低了,多加件衣服＿＿＿＿＿。

　　A．吧　　　　　　　　　　　B．了
　　C．呢　　　　　　　　　　　D．的

**题解：**正确答案是 A。这是一个祈使句,所以句子的末尾应该有一个表示祈使语气的助词。汉语普通话的语气助词有"吗"、"啊"、"吧"、"呢"、"了"、"呕"和它们的变体形式(如"啊"的变体"呀"、"哪"、"哇"等),其中表示祈使语气的助词是

"吧"。故选 A。

176. 她长得_____！

  A. 很漂亮极了      B. 非常漂亮极了

  C. 漂亮极了       D. 漂亮很极了

**题解**：正确答案是 C。程度副词和形容词结合可以用来表示程度，但是程度副词在和形容词结合的时候，或者出现在形容词之前，或者出现在形容词之后，不能同时出现在形容词的两端，所以 A、B 都可以排除。"很"和"极"都是程度副词，它们不能放在一起使用。所以 D 也是错的。

177. 他打算在这里_____。

  A. 多住几天      B. 多几天住

  C. 几天多住      D. 住多几天

**题解**：正确答案是 A。在普通话里，"多"作为形容词，在和动词、数量词组合的时候只有"多 + 动词 + 数量词"一种格式，表示比原来的数目有所增加，"多"做状语，如"多买一瓶"。当然在粤方言中大家接受的格式是"动词 + 多 + 数量词"，如"买多一瓶"。

178. 我一直想买这本书，可是_____。

  A. 买得不到      B. 买不得到

  C. 不买到       D. 买不到

**题解**：正确答案是 D。"动词 + 得 + 补语"是可能补语的肯定形式，可能补语的否定形式有两个："动词 + 不 + 补语"或者"没(有) + 动词 + 补语"，所以"买得到"和"买不到"都是合格的结构。根据句子的意思，这里应该是一个否定形式，那么只有"买不到"才是对的。

179. 这道题_____。

  A. 容易得很      B. 很容易得

  C. 非常容易得很     D. 容易得很非常

**题解**：正确答案是 A。程度副词和形容词结合可以用来表示程度，但是程度副词在和形容词结合的时候，或者出现在形容词之前，或者出现在形容词之后，不能同时出现在形容词的两端，所以 C 可以排除。"很"和"非常"都是程度副词，它们不能放在一起使用，所以 D 也是错的。在"形容词 + 得"表示程度的结构里，程度副词只能放在"得"字之后，因此 B 也是错的。

180. 别着急，有话_____。

  A. 很慢说       B. 说很慢

  C. 慢慢说       D. 说慢慢

**题解**：正确答案是 C。单音节形容词受"很"修饰后不能再做状语，也不能做光杆动词(bare verb)的补语，所以 A、B 都不能成立；单音节形容词重叠后可以做状语,如"满满斟了一杯酒",也可以做定语,如"满满一杯酒一口就喝干了",还可以加"的"以后做谓语、做补语,如"酒满满的"、"酒倒得满满的","慢慢"不带"的",只能放在动词前做状语,不能做补语,所以选择 C。

181. _____水果对身体有好处。
  A. 多吃一点儿     B. 一点儿多吃
  C. 多一点儿吃     D. 吃多一点儿

**题解**:正确答案是 A。在普通话里,"多"作为形容词,在和动词、数量词组合的时候只有"多+动词+数量词"一种格式,表示比原来的数目有所增加,"多"做状语。只有 A 符合这个格式的组合顺序。当然在粤方言中大家接受的格式是"动词+多+数量词"。

182. _____没关系。
  A. 一点儿天气冷    B. 天气一点儿冷
  C. 天气冷一点儿    D. 冷一点儿天气

**题解**:正确答案是 C。数量词"一点儿"在和动词、形容词搭配时只能放在动词、形容词之后,不能放在它们前边,据此可排除 A、B。当然我们有时可以看到"天气有一点儿冷"这样的例子,但是在这个例子里"一点儿"是接在动词"有"后面的,也就是说,"一点儿"跟"有"发生直接的结构关系,而与"冷"没有直接的结构关系。"动/形+(一)+点儿"表示程度数量略微增加或减少,数词限于"一","一"可省略,这个结构可以做主语,可以做谓语,但是不能做定语,做定语需加"的"。所以排除 D。这里"天气冷一点儿"是主谓短语,"冷一点儿"做"天气"的谓语。

183. 她_____。
  A. 很漂亮眼睛     B. 眼睛很漂亮
  C. 眼睛漂亮很     D. 很眼睛漂亮

**题解**:正确答案是 B。这是一个主谓谓语句。"很"是程度副词,它能够修饰像"漂亮"这样的形容词,但是不能修饰像"眼睛"这样的名词,故排除 D;也不能放在谓词后边做补语,如果要做补语必须有"得",这样就排除了 C。"很"修饰形容词之后不能直接修饰名词,除非加"的",所以 A 也是错的。

184. 这个电影_____。
  A. 我看过已经了    B. 看过我已经了
  C. 已经我看过了    D. 我已经看过了

**题解**:正确答案是 D。"已经"是一个表示"经历过"或"完结"的时间副词,其位置是主语成分之后,谓语成分之前,本句"看过了"是谓语成分,只有 D 符合"已经"出现的环境。这是个主谓谓语句。

185．她最近买了_____。

A．一辆红色的新汽车　　　　　B．一辆新红色的汽车

C．新红色一辆的汽车　　　　　D．红色新一辆的汽车

**题解**：正确答案是 A。这是一个多项定语的句子，多项定语的排列顺序是：(1)领属性名词、代词；(2)处所词与时间词；(3)数量短语；(4)主谓短语；(5)动词(短语)、介词短语；(6)形容词＋"的"；(7)不用"的"的形容词和描写性名词。本句定语的顺序是(3)(6)(7)。

186．这样做我觉得_____。

A．怎么不好　　　　　　　　　B．多么不好

C．不怎么好　　　　　　　　　D．不多么好

**题解**：正确答案是 C。"不＋怎么＋动/形"是一个固定搭配，"怎么"表示一定程度，略同于"很"而较轻。"怎么"的作用在于减弱"不"的力量，语气比较婉转，例如"不怎么好"没有"不好"坚决。

187．今天早晨她_____。

A．送给一束鲜花老师　　　　　B．送老师给一束鲜花

C．一束鲜花送老师给　　　　　D．送给老师一束鲜花

**题解**：正确答案是 D。动词"给"的使用条件是：V＋给＋间接宾语(接受者)＋直接宾语(接受对象)。只有 D 符合这个条件。

188．老师问你_____。

A．听懂了没有　　　　　　　　B．听没有懂了

C．有没有听懂了　　　　　　　D．听了懂没有

**题解**：正确答案是 A。"没有"是否定副词，用在问句形式中有两种格式：(1)"动/形(了)＋没有"，用于单纯提问，不作推测，A 符合这个条件。(2)"没有＋动/形＋吗"表示怀疑或惊讶，要求证实。问句形式也可以在句子中处于被包孕位置，做句子的成分。这个例子的问句形式就是处于被包孕状态。另外，"没有"不能在下面的环境中与"了"共现："没有＋动词/形容词＋了(le)"，所以 B、C 均应排除。

189．他_____地说："这事只有咱俩知道"。

A．不声音大　　　　　　　　　B．不大声音

C．声音大不　　　　　　　　　D．声音不大

**题解**：正确答案是 D。"不"是否定副词，出现在动词或者形容词前，这样就排除了 A、C。"不＋形容词"之后不能再修饰名词形成分，所以 B 也被排除。

190．请把这些书_____。

A．搬教室出　　　　　　　　　B．搬出教室

C．教室搬出　　　　　　　　　D．出教室搬

**题解:**正确答案是 B。趋向动词"出"出现的环境是:"动词 + 出 + 名词(处所)"或者"从 + 名词(处所) + 动词 + 补语"。只有 B 符合条件。

191. 他的学习成绩_____。

   A. 差多了  B. 多差了
   C. 差了多  D. 多了差

**题解:**正确答案是 A。"形 + 多 + 了"是一个固定搭配,这个格式可以表示:(1)程度比原来的基础上有所递增,如"她的病好多了";(2) 程度与某一参照标准相比有一定的距离,如"他的身高比要求矮多了"。

192. 这间屋子小,那间屋子比这间_____。

   A. 大多得  B. 大得多
   C. 多大得  D. 多得大

**题解:**正确答案是 B。"形 + 得 + 多"是一个固定搭配,用于比较句,表示相差的程度大,如"好得多"、"快得多"等。

193. 他让你在门口_____。

   A. 等一会儿  B. 一会儿等
   C. 等一点儿  D. 一点儿等

**题解:**正确答案是 A。"等"这样的动词如果带数量宾语的话要带表示时间的数量词语,"一点儿"不是表示时间的数量词语,排除 C、D。"一会儿"表示动作持续的时间短,但是它只能做"等"的宾语,不能出现在动词"等"之前。

194. 这本小说我_____。

   A. 看两遍过  B. 看过两遍
   C. 两遍看过  D. 过两遍看

**题解:**正确答案是 B。表示经验体的动态助词"过"只出现在动词或者述补结构后边,而且位置紧挨着动词或述补结构。这样只有 B、C 符合要求。如果出现在述宾结构里,"过"的位置在述语和宾语中间。数量词出现在动词之前必须是否定结构,而且数词限于"一"。如:"一遍也没看过"。C 不是否定结构,数词也不是"一",所以也被排除了。

195. 学校门口_____。

   A. 很多汽车有  B. 汽车很多有
   C. 有很多汽车  D. 有汽车很多

**题解:**正确答案是 C。"有"是表示领有、具有或存在的动词,如果句中的主语是一个人或者一个机构的话,"有"是表示领有的,如"学校有很多汽车",意思是"学校拥有很多汽车"。如果句子的主语是一个抽象词语的话,"有"表示具有某种属性或者某种结果,如"他的汉语水平有进步"。如果句子的主语是处所词语或者时间词语,"有"是表示存在的。这个句子中的"有"是表示存在的,表示存在的句子都有一个存在物和存在场所,构成"存在场所+有+存在物"的格式。这里只有C、D符合格式的要求。"很多汽车"是一个名词性成分,做"有"的宾语很自然。"汽车很多"是一个谓词性成分,做"有"的宾语不自然。

196. 现在的生活水平_____。

  A. 有了很大提高      B. 有提高很大了

  C. 很有大提高了      D. 很大有提高了

**题解**:正确答案是A。"有"是表示领有、具有或存在的动词,如果句中的主语是一个人或者一个机构的话,"有"是表示领有的,如"学校有很多汽车",意思是"学校拥有很多汽车"。如果句子的主语是一个抽象词语的话,"有"表示具有某种属性或者某种结果,如"他的汉语水平有进步"。如果句子的主语是处所词语或者时间词语,"有"是表示存在的。此处因为"生活水平"是抽象名词,"有"表示具有,"提高"做"有"的宾语,"很大"做"提高"的定语。

197. 公共汽车_____。

  A. 挤人满了       B. 挤满了人

  C. 挤了满人       D. 满挤了人

**题解**:正确答案是B。在现代汉语语法中,一个结构里如果既有宾语又有补语,组合的顺序是VCO(动词+补语+宾语),例如"吃饱饭",VOC(动词+宾语+补语)是不可接受的,例如"吃饭饱",因此A是不可接受的,B是可以接受的;一个结构里如果既有补语又有体标记的话,体标记出现在补语之后,如"VC了",而不能说"V了C",所以C也是不对的。形容词和动词共现除少数情况外,形容词总是在动词后边做补语,很少在动词前做状语,D也可以排除。

198. 那边_____小孩儿。

  A. 跑一个来       B. 一个跑来

  C. 来一个跑       D. 跑来一个

**题解**:正确答案是D。"小孩儿"是一个名词性成分,它的前边可以是及物动词,也可以是形容词、数量词,这个句子里只有一个不及物动词"跑",不可能出现在"小孩儿"前,所以能出现的只有D。

199. 那个学校_____学生。

  A. 一个死了       B. 死了一个

  C. 死一个了       D. 一个了死

**题解**:正确答案是B。"学生"是一个名词性成分,它的前边可以是及物动词,也可以是形容词、数量词,这个句子里只有一个不及物动词"死",不可能出现在"学生"前,所以能出现的只有B。

200. 站在门口的那个人_____王老师吗?

  A. 就不是        B. 不是就

  C. 不就是        D. 就是不

**题解:** 正确答案是 C。这是一种是非问句形式的反问句,这种反问句的格式是"不是……吗",如果有副词应该放在"是"前,意思是肯定的,带有明显的"事实如此"的语气。"就不是"是表示否定的,"不是就"、"就是不"后边应该出现谓词结构,因此这三个选择都被排除了。

# Keys to HSK Grammatical Section
# Class A (200 questions in total)

Fill in the blanks with the most suitable choice

## Time Words

1. The correct answer is C.

   According to the Chinese way of thinking, the order of things listed is generally arranged from the big to the small. In case of the time, the logic order is as follows: year, month, date, hour, minute and second, and in case of the place, the logic order is country, province, county, and township, etc. So the correct answer is C.

2. The correct answer is A.

   The explanation is the same as the above.

3. The correct answer is D.

   Chinese people usually place the bigger before the smaller. So in terms of the time words, first comes the year, then the month, date, hour, minute, and second. For this reason, answer C can be ruled out in the first place. In this question, "去年" modifies "今天", there existing between the two words the relationship of possession. So the auxiliary "的" between them cannot be omitted. Otherwise there would occur a logical conflict. Both "在……今天" and "在……这天" are prepositional structures and cannot be used as subjects. Therefore, neither A nor B is correct.

## Repeated Nouns

4. The correct answer is B.

   It is an idiom expressing good wishes. In Chinese, some nouns, used temporarily as quantifiers, could be overlapped to express universality, meaning "所有的……都(all and every one)". After being overlapped, they could only function as the subject of the sentence. "每" refers to each of the members within a certain collection, rather than all the members, emphasizing the sense of the individual.

5. The correct answer is A.

   The explanation is just the same as the above. The repeated nouns indicating time refer to the whole composing an aggregate, without exception. "一" and "每" cannot be used to refer to the whole.

## Pronoun

6. The correct answer is C.

   What is needed here is an adverbial, but "谁" and "什么" are substantive, and they have the same position in a sentence as nouns, that is they can be used as an object or subject, but not adverbial modifier. So answers A and B can be ruled out. Furthermore, this question is a rhetoric sentence, asking about the reason, while the answer "怎么样" asks about the ways of something being done, so the correct selection is C.

7. The correct answer is D.

What is needed here is an interrogative pronoun asking about the numbers, while "多" in answer C is an adjective. So answer C can be ruled out. "几" and "几个" are used to refer to a certain number within ten, and generally speaking, the number of the seats in a cinema can be anything but less than ten. So answers A and B can be ruled out. "多少" can be used to indicate any number without limits. Moreover, when "几" is used together with a noun, there is usually a measure word being inserted between them. In case of "多少", when it is used together with a noun, the presence or the absence of a measure word does not matter so much. So answer D is the correct one.

8. The correct answer is B.

What is lacking here is an attribute. When "谁" functions as an attribute, the structural auxiliary "的" is used to indicate the relationship of possession. So answer A can be ruled out. When "哪" is used, it is often followed by a measure word or a numeral-classifier compound. So answer C can also be ruled out. If "怎么" is used before "人", there should be the measure word "个" to be used together with it. And it is used to ask about the nature and the state. So answer D can be ruled out. "什么", when being used as an attribute to indicate the modifying relationship, is generally not followed by "的". Here "什么人" is used to indicate the relationship between "这位先生" and "你". So the correct answer is B.

9. The correct answer is A.

The explanation is just the same as the above. "谁", "怎么样" and "哪" must be followed by the structural auxiliary "的" when they are used as attributes to modify nouns.

10. The correct answer is A.

Among the four choices, only "哪" can be put before a measure word or a numeral-classifier compound. Moreover, "谁" is used to ask about somebody, "什么" is used to ask about something, and "怎么" is used to ask about the ways of something being done.

11. The correct answer is D.

What is needed here is an interrogative pronoun to ask about the ways that something is done or the conditions that something is in. "什么" is used to ask about something, and "哪里" is used to ask about the place. So answers B and C can be ruled out. When used as a predicate, "怎么" must be followed by "了" or another verb. So answer A can also be ruled out. "怎么样" is not necessarily followed either by "了" or another verb. So answer D should be chosen as the correct one.

12. The correct answer is B.

This is a declarative sentence and what is needed here is an adverbial. Neither "谁" nor "几" can be used for such a function. Although "怎么样" can be used as an adverbial, it is an interrogative pronoun, and should be used in a question. "多少" is an interrogative pronoun, but here it is used as an adverbial indicating "somewhat" or "more or less". So the only answer left is B.

13. The correct answer is A.

What is lacking here is an interrogative pronoun with a general reference used as an attribute for the reason that "苦" is used as a noun here, meaning "苦难,艰苦的经历 (a misery or a miserable experience)", and thus falling into the category of things. Among the four choices, only A is the best suitable one. "怎么" is used to refer to the ways that something is done and "多么" and "这么" are used to refer to the degree or the extent, and are generally used to modify the predicate word.

14. The correct answer is D.

"地方" is a noun falling into the scope of things and should be modified by demonstrative pronoun "什么". "几" is used to refer to quantity, and "怎么" is used to refer to ways that something is done. Neither of them is fit for the blank. Furthermore "哪里" is generally used to refer to a place or a position that are not certain, and "地方" also refers to a place or a position. So "哪里" and "地方" would be overlapped in their semantic sense, as a result of which, "哪里" cannot be used to modify "地方".

15. The correct answer is C.

"几" could be used either as an interrogative pronoun asking about quantity ranging from one to ten, or as an indefinite numeral indicating indefinite quantity ranging from one to ten. In the pattern of "系数词 + 位数词(digit numeral + place numeral)" which indicates quantity, it can be used to replace the digit numeral to indicate together with such place numerals as "十、百、千、万、亿" an approximate number larger than "二十 (twenty)", for example: "几十本书", "几十人" and "几百人" etc. "几多" is a dialect, indicating "多少(how many)". The only place numeral that can be collocated with "几个" is "亿". "多" is an adjective used to indicate a large quantity, rather than a pronoun referring to numbers.

16. The correct answer is B.

What is needed here is an indicative pronoun indicating the extent, but C and D are used to refer to places, so they can be ruled out. "那间教室" refers to the classroom away from here. Thus the best answer is B. We can say "这间教室没有那间教室那么大" on the one hand and "那间教室没有这间教室这么小" on the other hand.

17. The correct answer is C.

The character "些" in the phrase "这些" is a indefinite classifier, indicating an uncertain quantity. So there should be no definite numerals nor measure word following it. Thus A can be ruled out. "这儿" refers to places, and so B can also be ruled out. "哪" is an interrogative pronoun, and it could not be used in an imperative sentence. So it should be ruled out. When "这" is used together with a noun or "数量词 + 名词 (a classifier compound word + noun)", it can have a definite reference to both persons and things.

18. The correct answer is C.

In Chinese, such verbs as "来、去、到、上、回、在", etc. and such prepositions as "从、在", etc., are often followed by an object indicating a place. If the object is not a word indicating a place, but a personal noun or a noun with reference to a person or a thing, it must be followed by "这儿、那儿、这里、那里" to be changed into a place and used as an object. For example, "我从朋友那儿来". We cannot say "我从朋友来". "里" can only be put after such place nouns as "房子、礼堂、商店", etc. to indicate direction and position. "教师" is a noun referring to a person, and it cannot be followed immediately by "里". But we can say "老师肚子里有很多学问".

19. The correct answer is C.

"这会儿" has the meaning of "这个时候", referring to now or the present moment. It is often used after some words or expressions to indicate the definite time of just the present moment. "那会儿", however, refers to a time in the past or to come. So it can be ruled out according to the meaning of the sentence. "这时" and "那时" are often put at the beginning of a sentence, and when they are put in the middle of a sentence, they are often divided by a comma both before and after.

20. The correct answer is A.

The phrase "爱挑毛病" means "being ready to find faults of sb.", which is a predicate structure and could be preceded by an adverbial indicating the degree. "这么", an adverb, is often put before an adjective or a verb indicating psychological activities, suggesting the extent. "什么" is an interrogative pronoun with a reference of things, and cannot be used as an adverbial. Although "多么" is also an adverb indicating the extent, it can only be used in an exclamatory sentence and cannot be used in a rhetorical question. "要么" is a conjunctive indicating the relationship of selection.

21. The correct answer is B.

"那么" can be put before an approximate numeral indicating a certain estimation and in this case, they should be pronounced lightly. For example, "我们班有那么几个人对语法很有兴趣". "这些" and "那些" refer to things, and they have contained in them the implication of quantity. So they cannot be followed by other numeral-classifier compounds. "那里" is a word referring to places, and thus it should also be ruled out.

22. The correct answer is B.

"这么" or "那么" modifies predicative elements and can be the first to be ruled out. "这些或那些", "这样或那样" and "这里或那里" can all modify substantival words, but they are different in terms of meaning and usage. "这些或那些", as a modifier, cannot be followed by "的", and thus it can be ruled out. "这样或那样", as a modifier, must be followed by "的", and so it is the most suitable choice. "这里或那

里" refers to places, and it does not fit into the meaning of the question. So it should be ruled out.

23. The correct answer is D.

"去" means "to go to another place from where one is at the moment". "别的地方" should be referred to by a pronoun with a reference of being far away, that is, it should be like the pattern "去……那儿", while "来" is just the contrary, meaning to come to the speaker's place from another place and so should be referred to by a pronoun with a nearer reference, that is, it should be "来……这儿". So only D is correct.

24. The correct answer is B.

Only when being combined together with a measure word or a numeral-classifier compound, can "每" be put before nouns (with the exception of a few words such as "人" and "家", etc.). So A can be ruled out. Furthermore, "每个" lays more emphasis on the sense of taking out one or one group as an example, while "各" refers to every and all the individuals within a certain scope, laying more emphasis on concurrent and universal reference. So according to the meaning of the question, B should be the choice. "各民族" refers to all the peoples within the scope of "the whole nation" while "每个民族" refers to any one nationality of the nation.

25. The correct answer is B.

Only when being combined together with a measure word or a numeral-classifier compound can "每" be put before nouns (with the exception of a few words such as "人" and "家", etc.). So A can be ruled out. "到处" is an adverbial, and cannot be used as an attribute. "各个" cannot be used for modifying single syllable words. So only B should be chosen. Furthermore, "各地", "各省", "各民族" and "各学校" are commonly-seen collocations, meaning all the members within a certain group.

26. The correct answer is A.

"一本" is a numeral-classifier compound. So there is no need to put another measure word before it. Thus C and D can be ruled out. "各", as a demonstrative pronoun, can be put before a measure word, but not before a numeral-classifier compound. So B can also be ruled out. "每" often appears together with "都" in a sentence, denoting a sense of the whole. So A is the correct answer.

27. The correct answer is A.

"每" refers to any individual in a whole collection, emphasizing the sense of the whole composed of each individual. In a sentence where "每" is used, there often appears the adverb "都" to strengthen its sense. Both "时" and "刻" are quasi-measure-words, and "每" can be put before them. "每时每刻" is more like an idiom and "各时各刻" is not. That is to say we never say "各时各刻". The overlapping form of "时刻" is "时时刻刻" instead of "时刻时刻". So both A and B can be ruled out. "一时一刻" has no sense of all or the whole and it can also be ruled out.

28. The correct answer is D.

"每", as an adverb, means that the same action appears repeatedly and regularly, and it is often followed by "逢", "当" and "到" etc. "各" has no such usage. "当时", "at that time", refers to a certain time in the past. And if the action or behaviour in the sentence happened only once, we can say "当时我看见天边的彩霞,就想起了童年的你". But "就会" in the question tells us that what is indicated here is not a realistic and one-time action, but one that happened repeatedly. So the best answer is "每当".

29. The correct answer is A.

The reason is the same as Question 27. "一个" is a numeral classifier compound, and can neither be modified by "每每", which emphasizes that the same action happens repeatedly and regularly, nor by "各各", which has a meaning of universality. So C and D can be ruled out. "各", as a demonstrative pronoun, can be put before a measure word, but not before a numeral-classifier compound. Thus B can also be ruled out. "每" often appears together with "都" in a sentence, meaning universality. So A is the correct answer.

30. The correct answer is B.

"每", as an adverb, means that the same action happens repeatedly and regularly and is often followed by "逢", "当" and "到", etc. "各" has no such usage. Both "各个" and "每个" are often followed by a noun because of the measure word "个". So both C and D can be ruled out.

31. The correct answer is A.

"些" is a indefinite measure word meaning a certain amount of something and "有些" refers to some part of a group. The auxiliary word "的" could neither be put before nor after the word "些", and so there is no such saying as "有的些" and "有些的". "有的" also refers to a part of the whole. If "有的" and "一些" are used together, there would be semantic overlapping. So D is unacceptable and only A is correct.

32. The correct answer is C.

"别的" is a pronoun with reference to others, which can be used as an object and put after "有". None of A, B and D can be used as an object.

33. The correct answer is D.

"别人" is a pronoun with a general reference, meaning "all others except someone". "另外" and "其他" cannot be used as an object by itself without auxiliary "的" or a noun element. "谁" is an interrogative pronoun and "吗" is an interrogative modal particle, both indicating questioning. So they cannot appear simultaneously.

Adverb

34. The correct answer is B.

"那么(so)" could be put before an adjective to indicate the degree, for instance,

"天那么冷,他竟然不穿棉衣(The weather is that cold, yet he does not wear a coat)"。"那么、非常、十分"are all adverbials indicating the degree and should be used to precede the predicate elements, yet "勤劳、美丽、善良的人" is a noun phrase. Therefore, answers B, C, and D could not be used here.

35. The correct answer is B.

In Chinese, "verb + 不 + predicate elements (including adjective, verb or directional verb)" is a typical structure of predicate followed by a complement to express the inability of the subject to do something as well as the impossibility of something to be done. For example, "举不起", "听不清" and "看不见". Therefore, answers A and C could be ruled out just from the point of view of the grammatical pattern. In addition, the character "阅" is only a bound morpheme, rather than a word. So it should be ruled out also.

36. The correct answer is A.

The reason is the same as the above. In Chinese, "verb + 不 + predicate elements (including adjective, verb or directional verb)" is a typical structure of predicate followed by a complement to express the inability of the subject to do something as well as the impossibility of something to be done. For example, "拿不出来", "抬不进去", "看不出来" and "干不下去", etc. Thus, "不看进去" and "不进去看" could be ruled out just from the point of view of the grammatical pattern. The expression "进不去" is acceptable in terms of grammatical pattern, but when it is preceded by a verb, the structure would transform into "V + 不进去", rather than the pattern "V + 进不去".

37. The correct answer is A.

This is a special complement indicating possibility. Compared to the above-mentioned complements, it does not have its own corresponding affirmative form. For example, "来不及" has no corresponding affirmative form as "来及", as is applicable to "对不起——*对起" and "看不起——*看起". Such kinds of possibility complements are often closely combined with the verb preceding it and they have already been accepted as idiomatic structures. For example, "看不起" means "despising", "对不起" means "having a guilty conscience towards somebody else". Now that there is no such a pattern as "*看起", all the answers B, C and D could be ruled out.

Verbs

38. The correct answer is D.

The dynamic auxiliary "过" could be used after a verb and before a substantive object, which could be a noun phrase, pronoun, numeral and measure word, to mean that one has already experienced something. In case that the pattern of "用(use) + 工具名词(noun with reference to tools)" appears in the sentence, the verb could only be used after the pattern, otherwise the sentence would not be accepted. For this reason, answers A, B, and C are all wrong.

39. The correct answer is A.

B, C and D are all overlapping forms of the verb "打", indicating that the action concerned either lasts for relatively short time or happens less frequently or the time is not so certain. In the question, however, there are such words with reference to the time limits as "每天下午" and "两小时", which already gives a very clear definition of the time that the action lasts. So the only correct answer is A.

40. The correct answer is C.

The verb "旅游" in answer D is an intransitive one, and thus it could be ruled out in the first place. The verb "看望" in answer A could be followed only by the object with reference to persons whereas the object of "访问" in answer B can be a person, a city and a country (in the case of place names as objects, actually there would be certain individuals on their behalf to accept "访问"), etc., but not public places. Only the verb "参观" in answer C could take a public place as its object. So answer C should be chosen as the correct one.

41. The correct answer is B.

The Chinese "爱" is a verb that indicates human being's spiritual and psychological actions. It could not only take a substantive object, for instance, "爱孩子", but also a verbal one, for example, "爱听音乐". If there is an adverb indicating the extent used to modify the verb "爱", the adverb must be put in front of it instead of being after it. In this regard, answers A and D should be ruled out. When the adverb indicating the extreme extent "最" is used to modify the verb "爱", there should be no predicative element coming in front. So answer C should also be ruled out. Now the only correct answer left is "最爱喝绿茶" in answer B.

42. The correct answer is D.

In this sentence, the predicate here should be an action that has already happened, as could be concluded from the following result "没听见 (nothing was heard)". When "听" is used alone, there would be no time marker and accordingly it would be hard to decide whether the time is in the past, at present or in the future because there is no line of demarcation before and after the process it denotes. So answer A should be ruled out. What the phrase "听一听" indicates is an action that will happen, and thus it should also be ruled out. The pattern "听不听" is a selective question, which is not in accordance with the context and should be ruled out. And the pattern "听了听" is the only answer left, which indicates an action that has already completed.

43. The correct answer is A.

"喜欢" is a verb, and if there is an adverb to be used to modify it, that adverb should be put before it. So answer B, "喜欢非常", could be ruled out. Furthermore, in Chinese, there is no overlapping form for "喜欢" whether it is "喜喜欢欢" or "喜欢喜欢". So the only correct answer left is A.

44. The correct answer is B.

"进行" is a predicate-object verb, that is, it must be followed by a verbal object. If there is any prepositional structure or adverb to modify, it must be put in front of "进行". In this sentence, the prepositional structure "对她" and the time adverb "正在" are all modifiers using as adverbials, and thus both of them should be put in front of it. So answers A, C and D are all wrong.

45. The correct answer is C.

"希望" is a verb that could only be followed by a verbal object, which is in many cases a subject-predicate structure. "明年能够考上大学" is a subject-predicate structure, and so answer C should be chosen as the correct one. In addition, "希望" is a verb that could not be followed by the structural auxiliary word "了", so answer A is wrong. What is more, the verbal object that follows "希望" could not be the progressive or the perfect tense whereas "考上了" in answer B is the perfect one. So it is also wrong. Finally, "希望" could not be modified by such auxiliary verbs as "能", "愿意" and "乐意". Therefore, answer D is not the correct answer, either.

46. The correct answer is C.

The structure "可以让他给我做什么" is a pattern used to describe an event that will happen in the future, and thus it should not go with the overlapping form of "说了说", which suggests that something has been completed and realized. So answer A could be ruled out. Overlapping verbs could not be modified by "一" for the reason that the pattern "verb + 一 + verb" is the trial voice of the action, which means that the action would not be repeated or last for long. They could, however, be used to indicate that the action would last for short and could be repeated. The answer C "一说说" could not be accepted from the point of view of grammar. What the pattern "说一说" indicates is something that will happen in the future, which goes along well with the context of the question, and for this reason, answer C should be chosen as the correct one. Answer D "给我就说说" cannot stand, either, from the point of view of grammar because both "给我" and "就" are adverbials, and according to the traditional grammatical order of multiple adverbials in the Chinese language, adverbs should be put in front of the preposition structures, i.e., we could say "就给我说说," but not "给我就说说".

47. The correct answer is C.

In this sentence, the verb "研究" is a two-syllable one, and its overlapping form is "ABAB". For this reason, answer D could be ruled out first. There is no such overlapping form as "AB 一 AB" for two-syllable verbs. So "研究一研究" can be ruled out. For the reason that the auxiliary word "了" in the phrase "研究了研究" suggests the completion of the action, it goes against the "一起……吧" in the question, which indicates clearly that this is an imperative sentence. So answer B should also be ruled out.

48. The correct answer is D.

Here in this sentence, the modal verb "要" indicates a kind of requirement in terms of either reality or reason, meaning "应该(should)" used for conditions that have not been realized yet. Thus it is suitable for the question, and should be chosen as the correct one. Both "会" in answer A and "能" in answer B indicate the possibility of one's ability or the conditions, whereas "想" in answer C means "打算(plan, be going to do something)" expressing a kind of wish. None of them are in accordance with the context of the question.

49. The correct answer is D.

"不要" means "stop doing" or "unnecessary". So both A and B could be ruled out. "轻易(easily)" is the modifier of "得到(get)", not that of "会(would)", So answer C could also be ruled out. "不会" indicates a kind of inference, meaning "impossible". So answer D should be chosen as the correct one.

Auxiliary Word

50. The correct answer is C.

"估计" is a verb that must be followed by an object which is, in most cases, a sentence unless it is used as a parenthesis. "他不会来了" in answer C is a complete sentence in every sense and thus it could be put after the verb "估计". So the best answer is C. In addition, auxiliaries must be put directly before the verbal elements, without any elements in between. For this reason, answers A, B and D could all be ruled out.

51. The correct answer is D.

This is a question asking for the listener's opinion and it needs an auxiliary to indicate whether "准许(being allowed)" or not. So answer A, without an auxiliary, should be first ruled out. Only the auxiliary verb "能" indicates the meaning of being allowed both in subjective and objective terms. And what "要" and "会" indicate is a kind of probability or plan, with no meaning of "许可(being allowed)". So answer D should be chosen as the correct one.

52. The correct answer is B.

This is an interrogative sentence soliciting the listener's permission. "可能" in answer A indicates a kind of estimation, denoting the meaning of "perhaps" and "maybe". "应该" in answer C means "should, ought to" from the point of view of common sense, while "会" in answer D expresses the objective probability or the subjective ability. Only "可以" in answer B has the reference of allowing, and so B should be chosen as the correct one.

53. The correct answer is A.

This is an interrogative sentence asking about whether smoking is allowed. Among the four answers, only "能不能" in answer A indicates the meaning of "许可不许可(whether being allowed or not)". So the correct answer is A. "要不要" in answer B means "应该不应该 (whether it should be or should not be)" or "需要不需要 (whether it needs or does not need)", "会不会" in answer C asks about the possibility or the ability to do something, and "可能不可能" in answer D also asks about the possibility. Therefore none of them are in accordance with the context of the question.

54. The correct answer is B.

The auxiliary verb "得", pronounced as "děi" with the falling-rising tone, means "must, have to", indicating a kind of need from the reason. It is more affirmative than "应该(should, ought to)" and more colloquial. Both of "想" and "愿意" indicate a subjective wish and "会" indicates the objective probability or subjective ability. Thus only answer B is fit for the context of the question.

55. The correct answer is D.

Although according to Chinese grammar, some auxiliary verbs can be used together, the auxiliaries "可以", "能" and "会", all indicating probability, could not be used together since it will lead to overlapping in meaning and thus would be unacceptable. So answers A, B and C should all be ruled out.

56. The correct answer is B.

One of the grammatical features of auxiliary verbs is to use the juxtaposed pattern of affirmative and negative forms (for example, "能不能", "会不会" and "要不要", etc.) to make up selective questions. Another grammatical feature of auxiliary verbs is that when they are used as modifiers, they could only be put before the verb or the predicate structure. So answer D is wrong. What is more, the patterns like "能不能" could not be inserted in between. For this reason, answer C could be ruled out. In addition, what this sentence concerns is about the possibility and accordingly the suitable juxtaposed pattern of the affirmative and the negative should be "能", instead of "到". Thus answer A is not the correct one, and only B is right.

57. The correct answer is B.

It is known from the meaning of the question that this is a selective question, and the suitable way of expression should be the juxtaposed pattern of the affirmative and negative forms of the auxiliaries. In this way, answers C and D could be ruled out. "要不要" in answer A means "是否打算(whether intend or not)", or "是否应该(whether should or should not)", while "会不会" in answer B asks about the objective possibility or the subjective ability to do something. Thus according to the context of the sentence, answer B should be selected as the correct one.

58. The correct answer is D.

This is a yes-no question with a "把" pattern in it. Yes-no questions have the interrogative modal particle "吗" as their mark, which in turn forbids the use of the selective pattern of "能不能". So answer B should be ruled out. In the "把" pattern, the auxiliary verb and the negative adverb must be put in front of the character "把". So both answers A and C are wrong.

59. The correct answer is C.

"能不能" in answer C concerns about one's ability to do something or whether there is the objective possibility of doing something. Both of "可不可以" in answer A and "可以不可以" in answer B concern about whether the objective conditions permit something to be done. The meaning of "要不要" in answer D is "是否打算(whether one intends to do something or not)", "是否应该(whether one should do something or not)". Thus according to the context of the sentence, answer C should be chosen as the correct one.

60. The correct answer is C.

"要" is an auxiliary verb, indicating the intention or necessity to do something. The negative form is "不要", with the meaning of forbidding to do or dissuading somebody from doing something. What is needed here is just the words expressing the meaning of forbidding or dissuading. "不会" in answer A is the negation to "可能性(possibility)". "不想" in answer B means "not willing to" in subjective terms. The expression "不行" in answer D could only be used as an independent predicate element, rather than the adverbial before other predicate structures. So according to the meaning of the sentence, answer C should be chosen as the correct one.

61. The correct answer is B.

Here in this sentence, "无忧无虑地" is the adverbial modifying and restricting "活着", and "可以", an auxiliary verb, is the adverbial of "无忧无虑地活着". "可能" is an adverb, meaning estimation, which does not fit the meaning of the sentence. Thus both answers C and D should be ruled out. What is more, the expression "无忧无虑地" is an adverbial indicating a kind of state, whereas "可以" is an auxiliary verb and should be put before other adverbials when they are used together as an adverbial. Therefore, answer A should be ruled out and answer B should be chosen as the correct one.

62. The correct answer is C.

From the former half sentence "经理答应了", we could know that, before the phrase of "谈一谈", an auxiliary verb is needed to indicate permission or proposition. Only answer C meet this condition for the reason that the auxiliary "可以" has the meaning of permitting. Both "可能" and "会" indicate estimation, which does not go in accordance with the meaning of the sentence. So all of answers A, B and D should be ruled out.

63. The correct answer is D.

This is a complex sentence as well as a question asking about the possibility. The main structure of the sentence is "你妈妈……同意……吗?", and the object of "同意" is a subordinate clause "你嫁给他". The auxiliary verb "能" should be put before the main predicate verb "同意". Therefore, answers A, B, C should all be ruled out and answer D should be chosen as the correct one.

64. The correct answer is B.

From the former half sentence "今天作业太多", we could know that the following clause must be one that indicates possibility or willingness. The meaning of "不可以" in answer A is "不许可 (not allowing)", with the reference of forbidding, which does not go in accordance with the meaning of the sentence. "不能" in answer B means that the subjective ability or the objective condition do not allow something to be done, which just fits the sentence. So answer B should be chosen as the correct one. "不要" in answer C indicates forbidding or dissuading, and is not suitable for the meaning of the sentence. "不应该" in answer D means "should not do something" in the sense of reason, without the reference of possibility or willingness, and thus it should be ruled out.

65. The correct answer is A.

Although auxiliary verbs could be modified by adverbs, different auxiliary verbs have different requirements. "一定" could be used to modify "要", but not "应该". So answer C could be ruled out. Furthermore, "一定" is an adverb and must be put in front of the auxiliary verbs. So answers B and D should be ruled out as well.

66. The correct answer is C.

"会" has the following meanings: (1) "懂得做或有能力做某事 (know how to do something or have the ability of doing something)"; (2) "善于做某事 (be good at doing something)"; and (3) "有可能 (there is the possibility that something is done)". The meaning of "要" is "将要 (be going to do something)" or "打算 (planning to do something)". According to the meaning of the sentence, what the predicate means may be the plan of the subject. So both A and B could be ruled out. From another point of view, this sentence has three arguments: "他", "商店" and "一件大衣". The predicate is composed of "去" and "买". The auxiliary verb "要" modifies either "去" or "买", or "去……买", but not "买去". So answer D should be ruled out. The object of "去" is "商店", and the object of "买" is "一件大衣". And what "要" modifies is "去……买". In this way, only answer C meets the requirements.

67. The correct answer is B.

In this sentence, the verbal phrase "学会开汽车" is predicative, so the blank should be filled with an auxiliary verb. Since auxiliary verbs could not be reduplicated, answers A, C and D could all be ruled out.

The "的" Structure

68. The correct answer is B.

The structural auxiliary "的" could be used behind nouns, pronouns, adjectives, verbs, subject-predicate phrases and differentiating words, etc. to form the "的" phrase (the phrase ended with "的"), performing the function of a noun. "男" and "女" are differentiating words and they could not be used as a subject or an object independently. They can be a subject or an object only after they are changed into nouns by adding a "的" to them. Thus we can rule out answers A and D. "男的" and "女的" are classifying words which can only be used to refer to human beings and so it is not necessary to go the long way specially to point out it is a "男的人 (male human being)" or "女的人

(female human being)". Thus answer C could be ruled out as well.

69. The correct answer is A.

In the Chinese language, "小人" has a special reference, which is the opposite of "君子(the man of noble character)". In ancient times, it referred to a person with a humble position, and nowadays, it refers to a person with a mean character. So we should not take the words so literally as to take "小人" as "年幼的人(a very young person)". In this way, answers C and D can be ruled out. Moreover, in the semantic field of age, what is correspondent to "中年(middle-aged)" is: "老年(old-aged)", shortened as "老(old)", "青年(young-aged)", "少年(juvenile)", and "儿童(child)", whose shorter form is "小(little)". From the above, it could be seen that "老的" and "小的" have a referential character, referring specially to persons of a certain age, while "大" and "小" is only relative in its reference. So answer B can be ruled out. "上有老,下有小" is a idiomatic way of saying in the Chinese language.

70. The correct answer is C.

The overlapping form of one-syllabled adjectives cannot be used as predicates independently without the auxiliary "的" being put after it to become the "AA 的" pattern. After being reduplicated, an adjective indicates a kind of state, being given a meaning of extent. So it could not go together with the auxiliary "了", which has a very strong meaning of result. In this way, answer B is not correct. The "的" in answers A and D is a structural auxiliary. "红的" is a "的" structure, performing the function of a noun, and thus it cannot function independently as a predicate and could not be followed by the dynamic auxiliary "了", either. So both answers A and D could not stand.

## Adjectives

71. The correct answer is B.

The word "安静" can be used either as a verb or as an adjective. As a verb, its overlapping form is "安静安静(the ABAB pattern)". As an adjective, its overlapping form is "安安静静(the AABB pattern)". Here in this sentence, "安静" is a verb. So answer C can be ruled out, and answer B should be chosen as the correct one. Answers A and D are both forms that go against grammatical rules. So they should be ruled out also.

72. The correct answer is A.

The usage of "漂亮" is the same as that of "安静" in the sense that it can also be used either as a verb or as an adjective. As an adjective, its reduplicated form can be used as a predicate element only after the auxiliary "的" is added to it. Its reduplicated pattern itself cannot function as a predicate. So answer C can be ruled out. The reduplicated adjective cannot be modified by such adverbs indicating the degrees as "很" and "非常", etc. Thus answer B could be ruled out also. The character "让" in the sentence has the meaning of "使令(order, let or make somebody do)", which requires the following predicative element to be one indicating change or result instead of extent.

So "很漂亮" cannot be used. Answer A is the reduplicated form of verb used as a predicate. It goes well in accordance with the context of the sentence.

73. The correct answer is D.

"高兴" has the same usage as "安静" and "漂亮". Here in this sentence, it is used as an adverbial. Its correct reduplicated form should be AABB indicating the deep extent and there should be no adverbs before it indicating the degree. In this way, answer A should be ruled out. Furthermore, disyllabic adjectives are very rarely used as adverbials independently. And when they are used as adverbials, the auxiliary "地" should be added after them. Here in this sentence, answer D should be chosen as the correct one.

74. The correct answer is C.

"干净" is an adjective and is used here as a complement preceded by the structural auxiliary "得", indicating the result. Here in this sentence the correct reduplicated form of the adjective should be the pattern of AABB. So both answers A and B should be ruled out. Reduplicated adjectives can no more be modified by an adverb indicating the extent. In this way, answer D can also be ruled out and only C meets the context of the sentence.

75. The correct answer is C.

According to the phonic convenience principle of syllable collocation, monosyllabic adjectives are usually put before monosyllabic verbs as modifiers, for example, "高呼", "高喊", "大干" and "快上", etc. and disyllabic adjectives are usually put before disyllabic verbs or verbal phrases as modifiers (with the exception of imperative sentences), for example, "顽强抵抗", "坚决抵制", "成功发射" and "光荣退休", etc. In this sentence, the verb "举" is a monosyllabic one, and accordingly answer C should be chosen. Yet what should be noted is that not all adjectives can appear before a verb or verbal phrase as modifiers.

76. The correct answer is C.

"听课" is a disyllabic verbal structure. According to the phonic convenience principle of syllable collocation that we mentioned in question 75, there should be a disyllabic adjective before it as its modifier. The adjective "好" is an one-syllabled adjective and so it should be ruled out. After reduplicated, one-syllabled adjectives can function as adverbials. So "好好" in answer C meets the requirements. The reduplicated forms of adjectives in imperative sentences usually indicate a kind of imperative tone, for example, "慢慢说", "好好干" and "狠狠打他", etc. "很好" in answer B is a declarative structure, and could not be used in imperative sentences. So answer B should be ruled out. "好一好" in answer D is a wrong collocation for the reason that adjectives have no such reduplicated patterns as "A一A". So answer D is wrong.

## Numeral-classifier Compound Words

77. The correct answer is B.

Both "二" and "两" represent "2", but have different usages. Among the following place numerals "十、百、千、万、亿", "十、百" should use "二" to modify while before "千、万、亿", "两" should be used. In the combinations of digit and place numerals, the last number should use "二", for example, "十二", "一百零二" and "三百二". So in the above choices, only answer B meets this requirement.

78. The correct answer is A.

When "半" is used as a numeral, it can be put either before or after the measure word. If it appears together with other numerals, however, the following order should be followed: "other numerals + measure word + 半 + (noun)". Among the 4 answers, only A meets this requirement.

79. The correct answer is A.

When "零" is used as a numeral, it indicates the vacant case of a certain number. In the expression of numbers, if the digit numeral is vacant, "零" is used to make it up. For example, 30235 is "三万零二百三十五", and 23022 is "两万三千零二十二". "三万四千九百六十" is 34960, in which there is no vacant position for the numbers above 2 digits. So there is no need to fill the vacant position with "零".

80. The correct answer is A.

Here in this question, there are two issues involved. One is about the usage of "两" and "二", another is about the language order. Before the ordinal, fractional and decimal numbers, only "二" could be used, rather than "两". For example, "二年级", "二分之一" and "二点五", etc. In this way, answers B and D could be ruled out. According to the order of the Chinese language, which is usually arranged from the big to the small, answer C could be ruled out. Only A is correct.

81. The correct answer is D.

In the Chinese language, the verb always comes before the object. So answers B and C are all wrong. In addition, in the Chinese language, the attribute usually comes before the modified central element. Here "375" is the attribute of "汽车". So "375路汽车" is a grammatically correct collocation, while "汽车 375 路" is not. So answer A is not correct, either.

82. The correct answer is C.

According to the traditional Chinese way of thinking, the expression is from the big to the small. When speaking of the address, the logical order is "楼、门、号".

83. The correct answer is D.

The reason is just the same as the above. The logical order of time should be "年、月、日".

84. The correct answer is B.

In Chinese, numerals should be followed by measure words. So answers C and D can be ruled out. Whereas the numeral before the measure word "个" should be "两" instead of "二". Thus answer B should be chosen as the correct one.

85. The correct answer is C.

Both "二" and "两" mean "two", but have different usages. Among the following digit numerals: "十、百、千、万、亿", "二" should be used only before "十、百" while before "千、万、亿", "两" should be used. In the combinations of digit and place numerals, the last of the number should use "二" to express "2", for example, "十二", "一百零二" and "三百二". So in the above choices, only answer C meets this requirement.

86. The correct answer is D.

The cardinal numerals in the Chinese language are divided into digit and place numerals. The digit numerals of the integers are one, two, three, four, five, six, seven, eight, nine and ten. And the place numerals are ten, hundred, thousand, ten thousand, and hundred million etc. Among the above, ten is both a digit and a place numeral. The Chinese language uses the decimal system to make the calculations. When the number is less than ten thousand, the digit is no more than ten. If it is more than ten, it will carry. So it is wrong to say "十五千". The correct saying is "一万五千". In this way, both answers A and B should be ruled out. "多", indicating an approximate number, can only be put after a place numeral, for example, "二百多", "两万多", etc. It is wrong to say "二多百" and "两多万". So only answer D is correct.

87. The correct answer is B.

When two neibouring numerals are used together, they could indicate an approximate number. Generally speaking, it is usually the coefficient numerals, and usually the smaller number is put in the front, and the bigger one is put in the behind, for example, "八九个" and "十五六个". In this way, answer D can be ruled out. The exception is "九" and "十", which cannot be used together to indicate an approximate number. The numerals that can be used together with "几" to indicate an approximate number are only limited to those round numbers above ten and below a hundred, for example, "十几天" and "二十几年". It cannot be used together with those numerals that are not round numbers, for example it is wrong to say "五几天" and "十四几天". So A is wrong. "十几" is already indicating the approximation, and "多" has the same meaning. There would appear a repeat of the meaning if they are used together. So C is wrong also.

88. The correct answer is D.

Numerals above ten can be used together to indicate an approximate number. The two neibouring numerals after being used together need only one digit numeral after them. In this way, A can be ruled out. The order of the numerals used together is that the smaller one comes before the larger one, for example: "八九十" and "五六百". Answer D meets this requirement. Cardinal numerals used together are already indicating approximation, and "多" also has such a meaning. Their being used together would cause a repeating of meaning. So answers B and C are both wrong.

89. The correct answer is C.

"多", when used after a numeral, indicates that the remaining sum beyond the round figure is indefinite. Its position and usage is as follows: 1. a numeral + "多" + a measure word ( + a noun). Here the numeral must be a round number that is above ten (including ten), for example: "十多斤(苹果)" and "一百多个(学生)". Obviously, all the four answers do not belong to this category; 2. a numeral + a measure word + "多" ( + a noun). The numerals used this way must be those cardinal ones that range from one to ten (including "两"). Among the four answers here, only C meets the requirements.

90. The correct answer is B.

"多", when used after a numeral, indicates that the remaining sum beyond the round figure is indefinite. Its position and usage is as follows: 1. a numeral + "多" + a measure word ( + a noun). Here the numeral must be a round number that is above ten (including ten), for example: "十多斤(苹果)" and "一百多个(学生)". Obviously, all the four answers do not belong to this category; 2. a numeral + a measure word + "多" ( + a noun). The numerals used this way must be those cardinal ones that range from one to ten (including "两"). Among the four answers here, only B meets the requirements.

91. The correct answer is B.

When "几", as an approximate numeral word, indicates an indefinite number, it is generally followed by a measure word or a noun used temporarily as a measure word (for example, "几天" and "几年") unless it is asking about the age (for example: "他今年二十几了?"). Both answers A and C have no measure word after them. So they can be ruled out. "人" in answer D is not a temporary measure word. So it can also be ruled out.

92. The correct answer is B.

In the phrases expressing numbers, "几" can be used to take the place of a digit numeral, indicating an approximate number below ten (not including ten), for example, "十几本书", "几十个人" and "几百人". The numerals that are used together with "几" are limited only to those place numerals of the round numbers (for example: "十", "百" and "千", etc.). "十五" in answer A is not round number, and so answer A does not meet this requirement. "多", also indicating the approximate number, should not be used after other numerals indicating the approximate number. In this way, both answers C and D can be ruled out.

93. The correct answer is C.

The usual way of saying a fractional number is "X 分之 Y", in which, X indicates the denominator, and the following Y indicates the numerator. For example, 2/3 is pronounced as "三分之二". So both A and B are wrong. There is no grammatical error in answer A, but to our common sense, it does not tally with meaning of this sentence, and so it is also wrong.

94. The correct answer is D.

The way of expressing percentage is "百分之 X". Both of answers B and C are against this requirement. The usual way of speaking a fractional number is to pronounce the decimal point as "点(point)", and those numbers following the decimal point as digit numerals. For example, "3.1416" is pronounced as "三点一四一六". Only answer D meets this requirement.

95. The correct answer is C.

If there is no whole number, the numeral "半" is put before the measure word, for example: "半斤", "半个" and "半尺", whereas if there is a whole number, "半" is put after the measure word and can be followed by a noun, which can also be omitted. For example: "一斤半(肉)", and "一里半(地)". There is no measure word in answer A, while in both answers B and D, the measure word "一" should not be there. Only C is correct.

96. The correct answer is A.

According to the explanation in Question 95, B and D should be ruled out. Here in this sentence, "已经" is used as the adverbial of "三年半了", and should be put in front of it. So A is the correct answer.

97. The correct answer is C.

The unit of the current Chinese money Renminbi is Yuan (also called "块"[kuai] in spoken language), Jiao (also called "毛"[mao] in spoken language), and fen. The decimal system is adopted, that is, 10 fens equals to one jiao (mao), and 10 jiaos (mao) equals to one yuan (kuai). There is no "零" used between two neibouring units, for example, 5.55 yuan is pronounced as "五块五毛五" instead of "五块零五毛五". "零" is used only between two units that are not next to each other, for example, 5.05 should be read as "五块零五分".

98. The correct answer is A.

The unit of the current Chinese money Renminbi is Yuan (also called "块"[kuai] in spoken language), Jiao (also called "毛"[mao] in spoken language), and fen. The decimal system is adopted, that is, 10 fens equals to one jiao (mao), and 10 jiaos (mao) equals to one yuan (kuai). There is no "零" used between two neibouring units, for example, 5.55 yuan is pronounced as "五块五毛五" instead of "五块零五毛五". "零" is used only between two units that are not next to each other, for example, 5.05 should be read as "五块零五分". So both answers B and D are wrong. For the reason that it is a decimal system, there is no such saying as "五十分". So answer C is also wrong.

99. The correct answer is B.

In Chinese, the way to speak numbers 11-19 is "十一, 十二……十八, 十九". It is not necessary to take the trouble to speak "一十一, 一十二……一十八, 一十九", that is to say, the "一" before "十" can be omitted. But if it is a number that has more than two digits, "一" can not be omitted. For example, 318 should be read as

"三百一十八". So answer B is wrong. One usage of "零" is to make up the vacant position of a place numeral. For example, 308 should be read as "三百零八". If there is no such vacant positions, "零" is not used. So both answers C and D are wrong.

## Measure Words

100. The correct answer is D.

Individual nouns have their own particular measure words to be used after. For example, when speaking of books, the measure word is "本", and when speaking of "床", the measure word is "张". Sometimes, there is a kind of linkage in meaning between the noun and the measure word that matches it, but this is only a rare situation. The matching between the noun and the measure word is usually a well-formed common practice. For instance, both measure words "本" and "部" can be used with "词典", but not others.

101. The correct answer is C.

The reason is the same as that of Question 100. Generally speaking, if the thing in question has a surface that is smooth and extendable, the measure word is "张", and if it has a handle, the measure word is usually "把", and the shirt is usually spoken of by "件".

102. The correct answer is B.

The reason is the same as that of Question 100. All of the measure words in the four choices could be used together with nouns with a reference of human being, but only the measure word "位" could be used in such addressing expressions as "几位,您几位,你们三位" to show respect and courtesy.

103. The correct answer is C.

The reason is the same as that of Question 100. The measure word "所" is often collocated with such nouns as "学校" and "医院", etc. And "座" is usually matched with "房子", "院落", "工厂" and "山". "件" is often used together with such words as "衣服", "礼物" and "事". "间" is usually used together with such words as "屋子" and "卧室", etc.

104. The correct answer is C.

The reason is the same as that of Question 100. "课" is often collocated with "课文", "条" is often used together with a thing that has a rectangular shape, and "支" is generally matched with such words as "笔" and "队伍", etc. The measure word that goes together with "树" is "棵".

105. The correct answer is D.

"位" is collocated with a noun referring to a person. When animals like "鸭子" is spoken of, the unit is "只".

106. The correct answer is A.

The reason is the same as that of Question 100. "口", as a measure word, can be used together with "人", indicating the number of the people. It can also be used together with such nouns as "井" and "锅", etc, indicating the number. "名", as a measure word, is usually used before a person that has some status. "头", as a measure word, is used together with such nouns as "猪" and "大蒜". "位", as a measure word, goes together with such nouns referring to human beings as "客人" and "小姐", etc, indicating respect, but it cannot be used together with "人".

107. The correct answer is B.

"位", as a measure word, goes together with such nouns as "客人" and "小姐", etc, indicating respect. "条" is collocated with things that have a rectangular shape or is collocated with abstract words such as "意见,建议", etc. "件" is used together with such nouns as "衣服" and "事", etc. The measure word used together with the noun "椅子" is "把".

108. The correct answer is C.

The reduplicated numeral-classifier compounds could be used as the subject to emphasize the characteristic of being universal, without any exception, of the whole group that is composed of each individual "每个", and "每一个" refers to the individuals that make up the entire collection. If they are used to stress the universality of the whole group that is composed by the individuals, there must be an adverb "都" to be used after them. "一个" could only be used to indicate individuals. So according to the meaning of the question, answer C should be chosen as the correct one.

109. The correct answer is A.

The measure words could be reduplicated to indicate the universality of the entire collection that is composed of each individual, with no exception. After being reduplicated, it can be and can only be modified by the numeral "一". So answer A should be chosen and C should be ruled out. "孩子们的……笑脸" is plural, and so answer D can be ruled out. "张" can not be modified by the indefinite measure word "些".

110. The correct answer is B.

The reduplicated numeral-classifier compounds could be used either as the subject or the attribute to indicate the universality of the entire collection that is composed of each individual, with no exception. "每条" and "每一条" refer to the individuals that make up the entire collection. If it is used to indicate the entire collection that is composed of individuals, there must be an adverb "都" to be used after to indicate the universality. "所有" should have a noun after it, and could not be used to modify the measure word "条" directly. Moreover, "条条大路通罗马" is an idiom.

111. The correct answer is C.

The reduplicated numeral-classifier compounds could be used as the subject or the attribute to indicate the universality of the entire collection that is composed of each individual, with no exception. "每种" and "每一种" refer to the individuals that make up the entire collection. If it is used to indicate the entire collection that is composed of the individuals, there must be an adverb "都" to be used after to indicate the universality. So both answers A and B can be ruled out. A measure word after being reduplicated can not be modified by "每". So answer D can also be ruled out.

112. The correct answer is B.

"遍", "次", "下" and "阵" are all verbal measure words. The word "遍" refers to the whole process of an action or a set of actions from the beginning to the end, for example, "再讲一遍这个故事". "次" expresses the frequency of a behaviour or an action, and is often used to refer to something that appears repeatedly, for example, "去了三次". "下" indicates the times an action happens, and is generally used to refer to actions that last shortly. "一下" also has the function of softening the tone. "阵" indicates an action that could last, for example, "一阵猛打". According to the context of the question, answer B should be chosen as the correct one.

113. The correct answer is C.

The verbal measure word "趟" generally refers to the number of times that one goes away and comes back. "回" refers to the number of times of an action that happens, and it is also used for actions that happen repeatedly, and it is more colloquial than "次". "阵" indicates an action that can last, for example, "一阵猛打". "遍" refers to the whole process of an action or a set of actions from the beginning to the end, for example, "再讲一遍这个故事". According to the meaning of the sentence, answer C should be chosen as the correct one.

114. The correct answer is D.

"口", as a temporarily used verbal measure word, indicates the number of the times of the oral movement. Its usage is as follows: (1) a verb + a numeral + "口", for example: "被蛇咬了一口"; (2) a numeral + "口" + a verb, for example, "一口吞下". Usage (1) is suitable for the sentence in question here. "一大" can only be used to modify temporarily-used measure words concerning a certain part of the body, for example: "踢一大脚" and "打一大嘴巴". So the correct answer for the question should be D.

115. The correct answer is B.

"次", "下", "遍" and "趟" are all verbal measure words. "次" refers to the number of times of an action or behaviour that happens, and is generally used for things that appear repeatedly, for example: "去了三次". "下" refers to the number of times of an action that happens, and is generally used for things that last very shortly. "一下" has the function of softening the tone. "遍" emphasizes the whole process of an action or a set of actions from the beginning to the end, for example, "再讲一遍这个故事". "趟" indicates the number of times that one goes away and comes back, for example, "去一趟银行". According to the context of the question, answer B should be chosen as the correct one because "不小心撞了她" could not be a set of actions or repeat again and again, but an action that lasts for a very short time. Here in this sentence, "一下" has the function of softening the tone.

## Negative Adverbs

116. The correct answer is B.

"不", "没(有)", "别" and "甭" are all negative adverbs. They can be put either before a verb or an adjective to negate the action or the state, but their usages are different. When modifying a verb, "不" is used to negate the judgement or one's wish, and what it negates has nothing to do with the time feature, that is, what is negatived can be the judgement or the wish of the present, the future or the past. "没(有)" is a negation of a behaviour or an action that has already been the case. What is negatived is a thing that has already happened. "别" and "甭" indicates dissuasion and forbidding. According to the context of the question, what is negatived here is an action that has already happened. So answer B should be chosen as the correct one.

117. The correct answer is A.

"不", "没", "没有" and "别" are all negative adverbs. They can be put before either a verb or an adjective, to negate the action or the state, and their usages are different. When modifying a verb, "不" is used to negate the judgement or one's wish, and what it negates has nothing to do with the time feature, that is, what is negatived can be that of the present, the future or the past. "没(有)" is a negation of a behaviour or an action that has already been the case. What it negates is something that has already happened. "别" indicates dissuasion and forbidding. According to the context of the question, what is negatived here is a wish that has not happened yet. So answer A should be chosen as the correct one.

118. The correct answer is C.

"不", "没", "没有" and "别" are all negative adverbs. They can be put either before a verb or an adjective to negate the action or the state, and their usages are different. When modifying a verb, "不" is used to negate the judgement or one's wish, and what it negates has nothing to do with the time feature, that is, what is negatived can be the judgement or the wish of the present, the future or the past. "没(有)" is a negation of a behaviour or an action that has already been the case. What it negates is something that has already happened. "别" indicates dissuasion and forbidding. According to the context of the question, the tone here indicates dissuasion. So answer C should be chosen as the correct one.

119. The correct answer is C.

"英语说得好不好" is a kind of comment. In the Chinese language, when describing, commenting, or judging an action, the pattern "得 + an adjective phrase or an adjective" is generally used. If the description, commenting or judging is negative, the negative word is generally put after "得" but before the adjective or the adjective phrase.

Whereas making comments to a certain kind of state, "不" should be used. So answer C should be chosen. "说得好" is a predicative-complement structure indicating result or possibility. There is only one form of negation for it, that is "说得不好", whose structure is "V + 得 + Neg. + A", instead of "Neg. + V + 得 + A". So both answers A and B are wrong.

120. The correct answer is C.

"不", "没", "没有" and "别" are all negative adverbs. They can be put before a verb or an adjective to negate the action or the state, but their usages are different. When modifying a verb, "不" is used to negate the judgement or one's wish, and what it negates has nothing to do with the time feature, that is, what is negatived can be that of the present, the future and the past. "没(有)" is a negation of a behaviour or an action that has already been the case. What it negates is something that has already happened. "别" indicates dissuasion and forbidding. According to the context of the question, this is a sentence giving judgement to something that has already happened, and what is negated here is the action of "去" which is something that has already taken place. So answer A should be ruled out. This is not a sentence indicating dissuasion or forbidding, and thus answer D can also be ruled out. When "没" is used together with other adverbs, it can only be put in front of them. So answer C should be chosen as the correct one.

121. The correct answer is D.

"不", "没", "没有" and "别" are all negative adverbs. They can be put before a verb or an adjective to negate the action or the state, but their usages are different. When modifying a verb, "不" is used to negate the judgement or one's wish, and what it negates has nothing to do with the time feature, that is, what is negatived can be that of the present, the future and the past. "没(有)" is a negation of a behaviour or an action that has already been the case. What it negates is something that has already happened. "别" indicates dissuasion and forbidding. What is mentioned in this sentence is something that will happen "明天上午(tomorrow morning)", So "没" in answer A and "没有" in answer B can be ruled out. And what is spoken here is something of "我(myself)", and it is not a dissuasion. So "别" in answer C can be ruled out. And the only answer left is "不" in answer D, which negates a wish.

122. The correct answer is A.

"不", "没", "没有" and "别" are all negative adverbs. They can be put before a verb or an adjective to negate the action or the state. They have different usages. When modifying an adjective, "不" negates the nature, whereas "没(有)" is a negation of a behaviour or an action that has already been the case. When "没有" modifying ajectives, the adjectives must be dynamic words that indicate changes instead of static words indicating the nature or state. "别" indicates dissuasion and forbidding. "漂亮" is a static nature, and can only be negated by "不".

123. The correct answer is D.

"不","没",and "没有" are all negative adverbs. They can be put before a verb or an adjective to negate the action or the state. They have different usages. When modifying a verb, "不" negates the judgement or one's wish, and what it negates has nothing to do with the time feature, that is, what is negatived can be that of the present, the future and the past. "没(有)" is a negation of a behaviour or action that has already been the case. What it negates is a thing that has already happened. According to the context of the question, what is expressed here is a wish. So "不" should be used and answer D should be chosen. Moreover, it is only under certain conditions that the negative adverb "没有"can coexist with the modal particle "了", which is usually at the end of the sentence. That is, there should be such words as "好久" and "三个星期", etc in the front, which indicate a certain limited period of time. In this sentence, there is no such words. So answers A and B should be ruled out.

**124. The correct answer is B.**

"不","没","没有" and "别" are all negative adverbs. They can be put before a verb or an adjective to negate the action or the state. They have different usages. When modifying a verb, "不" negates the judgement or one's wish, and what it negates has nothing to do with the time feature, that is, what is negatived can be that of the present, the future and the past. "没(有)" is a negation of a behaviour or action that has already been the case. What it negates is a thing that has already happened. "别" indicates dissuasion and forbidding. Obviously, this sentence indicates dissuasion. So "别" in answer B should be chosen.

**125. The correct answer is A.**

"不","没","没有" and "别" are all negative adverbs. They can be put before a verb or an adjective to negate the action or the state. They have different usages. When modifying a verb, "不" negates the judgement or one's wish, and what it negates has nothing to do with the time feature, that is, what is negatived can be that of the present, the future and the past. "没(有)" is a negation of a behaviour or action that has already been the case. What it negates is a thing that has already happened. "别" indicates dissuasion and forbidding. "早" is a kind of state, and should be negated by "不". Furthermore, it is only under certain conditions that the negative adverb "没有"can coexist with the modal particle "了" appearing at the end of the sentence, that is, there should be such words as "好久" and "三个星期", etc. in the front to indicate a certain limited period of time. In this sentence, there is no such expression appearing. So "没" and "没有" should be ruled out. The first sub-sentence in this question does not indicate dissuasion, but judgement. So "别" cannot be used and "不" should be chosen as the correct answer.

## Time Adverbs

**126. The correct answer is C.**

"才" is a time adverb, and is generally used to express the speaker's opinion about the lateness or slowness of the action concerned. When thus used, there must be a word or phrase in front of it to indicate the time unless it is used in an interrogative sentence. "才" should be put after the subject and before the verb. So answer C should be chosen.

127. The correct answer is A.

"就", as a time adverb, is generally used to introduce the second action or behaviour of the two actions or behaviours that happen exactly one after the other, and it is usually put before the verb and after the subject. So answer A should be chosen.

128. The correct answer is C.

"就" and "才" are both time adverbs, and they usually precede actions or things that are related to a certain specific time. "总" and "常" can also indicate time, but what they indicate are usually actions, behaviours or events that happen commonly. What this sentence is talking about is an event that is related to a certain concrete time. So answers B and D should be ruled out. What is meant by "才" is that the speaker thinks that the behaviour or the action comes too slow or late. The meaning of "就" is just the contrary. It means that the speaker thinks that the behaviour or the action comes too early or quickly. In this sentence, "两个小时" is a long time in the speaker's opinion. So "才" should be chosen.

129. The correct answer is B.

"才" in this sentence is a relative adverb used in the second subsentence of a compound, indicating that a certain result comes out only under a certain condition or reason. In the former subsentence, there are usually such relative words as "只有、必须、要、因为、由于、为了" that are correspondent with it. "常常" is a frequency adverb. "正在" is a time adverb, indicating that the action or the state is going on. According to the context of the question, the relative adverb "才" should be chosen. "就" and "才" are contrary in their meaning, and they could not be used together. So answer A should be ruled out.

130. The correct answer is C.

"曾经", "已经", "经常" and "刚" are all adverbs that are related to time. "曾经" means that a certain action or situation that once existed in the past, and is generally used together with the auxiliary "过", for example: "我曾经当过老师". "已经" indicates that the action or the event concerned has already completed, and the time of completion is not long ago and its influence could still be felt at present time. "经常" is a frequency adverb, indicating that an action or behaviour happens often. The adverb can be used to modify things that happen frequently in a certain period of time passed or habitual things that has lasted till the present time. "刚" indicates something happened in a past time, but very near the moment of speaking. They must be put before the verb to function as an adverbial. For this reason, only answer C meets the requirements.

131. The correct answer is B.

"常常", "已经", "正在" and "曾经" are all adverbs related to time. "常常" is a frequency adverb, indicating that an action or behaviour happens often in a certain period of time passed or habitual things that has lasted till the present time. "已经" indicates that the action or the event concerned has already completed, and the time of completion is not long ago and its influence could still be felt at the present time. "正在" is a time adverb, indicating the action or the state is going on. The modal particle "了" at the end of this sentence indicates a kind of result, and is generally correspondent in meaning with "已经", indicating completion. So answer B should be chosen as the correct one.

## Scope Adverbs

132. The correct answer is D.

"都", as a scope adverb, indicates that everyone is included in a certain group. Except in questions, all the objects to be included in must be put in front of it. In this way, both answers A and B can be ruled out. In terms of the syntax, "都" is used to modify the verbs or adjectives that follows, indicating that the things it defines all happen without the exception or all have the features described by the predicative verb or the adjective. Only answer D meets the requirements concerned.

133. The correct answer is C.

"都" and "向她" are both adverbials in this sentence and they should be put in front of the verb "祝贺". So both B and D could be ruled out. When "都" is used with a preposition structure simultaneously as adverbials, it is always the nearest to the verb for it cannot be separated from the elements it modifies. So answer A is wrong.

134. The correct answer is B.

"只" and "都" are both scope adverbs. "只" indicates a limited scope and "都" indicates the whole. The object defined by "只" is behind it, for example: "只有一个孩子", while the object defined by "都" is put before it, and the object could not be a singular noun, for example: "他们都来了". "我" is a singular, and so it cannot be modified by "都". So answers C and D can be ruled out. From the view of syntax, adverbs are used to modify the verbs following it. According to the meaning of the question, "只" here in this sentence modifies the verbal phrase "想帮助你". So answer B should be chosen. If the second part of the sentence is changed, for example, into "我想只帮助你,不帮助别人", then "只" here governs "你". In this case, answer A could be chosen.

135. The correct answer is C.

"一共" is also an adverb indicating the scope, and it is put before the verb to function as an adverbial. Under this condition, there is always a numeral-classifier compound as the object of the verb. In this sentence, it is only in answer C that "一共" is put before the verb, and so answer C should be chosen as the correct one.

## Extent Adverbs

**136. The correct answer is D.**

As an extent adverb, "很" is used before an adjective. So answer A could be ruled out. "很 + adjective" cannot be put before a verb or a verbal structure to function as an adverbial. In this way, answer B can be ruled out. "很 + adjective" can function as a predicate, illustrating a substantive topic. "下雪" is predicative, with an adverb "还" as its modifier, and it cannot be the topic of the phrase "很大". So answer C can also be ruled out. The structure "很 + adjective + 的" can modify a noun. So answer D should be chosen as the correct one.

**137. The correct answer is A.**

"太", "很", "非常" and "十分" are all extent adverbs, but they are very different in terms of the extent and their concrete usage. "太 + (不) + adjective + 了" is a fixed collocation.

**138. The correct answer is C.**

"多么" is an extent adverb, indicating a very high degree. It is featured with an exaggerated tone and a strong passion, and is often used in such exclamatory sentences as (1) "多么 + adjective/verb", and (2) "多么 + 不 + adjective/verb". At the end of such sentences, there are usually such words as "啊(呀、哪、哇)". "很" is also an extent adverb, but the extent it indicates is not so strong as "多么". Those extent adverbs cannot be used to modify and restrict an adjective at the same time. So both answers A and B can be ruled out. In terms of the syntactic position, "多么" can only be put before a verb or a verbal structure to function as an adverbial. Thus answer D could also be ruled out. Only answer C is correct.

**139. The correct answer is D.**

"非常" is an extent adverb, indicating a very high degree. "极" is also an extent adverb. But they have different usages. Both "非常" and "极" can function as an adverbial, but the structure "极 + 了" often functions as a complement while the adverb "非常" has no such usage. The two extent adverbs cannot be used to modify and restrict an adjective at the same time. So all answers A, B and C can be ruled out.

**140. The correct answer is C.**

The interrogative form of "the extent adverb + adjective" used as a predicate are only limited to questions with special reference, except alternative questions. So all answers A, B and D are wrong, and C should be chosen.

**141. The correct answer is A.**

"多", "很", "更" and "太" are all extent adverbs, but they are different in terms of the extent and usage. "多" is featured with an exaggerated tone and a strong passion, and it is often used in an exclamatory sentence, forming the pattern "多 + (不) adjective". At the end of such sentences, there are usually modal particles like "啊(呀、哪、哇)" corresponding with it, whereas the adverbs "很" and "更" have no such usages.

The adverb "太" is also featured with an exaggerated tone and a strong passion, but in an exclamatory sentence, the modal particle that corresponds with the pattern "太 + (不) adjective" is "啦". In this sentence, the modal particle at the end of the sentence is "呀". So answer A should be chosen as the correct one.

## Relative Adverbs

142. The correct answer is B.

"再", "又", "还" and "也" are all relative adverbs that can be used to indicate the repeat, recurrence or continuity of an action or behaviour. When indicating a recurrent or continuous action, both of "再" and "还" refer to actions to be realized, and "又" expresses actions that have already come true. The difference between the adverbs "也" and "又" is that "也" indicates similarity, meaning that the same action or state has happened to another different object. So when "也" is used, there should be a comparable item. "又" indicates repeat and recurrence, meaning that the same kind of action or behaviour has happened to the same object. According to the meaning of the sentence, "刚说完(talked about just now)" and "提起(mention)" belong to the same kind of action. So "又" should be chosen. Here in this sentence, "又" indicates the repeat or recurrence of the same action, with the tone of reproach or dissatisfaction.

143. The correct answer is A.

"再", "又", "还" and "也" are all relative adverbs that can be used to indicate the repeat, recurrence or continuity of an action or behaviour. When indicating a recurrent or continuous action, both of "再" and "还" refer to actions to be realized, and "又" expresses actions that have already come true. "想" is a modal verb that indicates planning or willingness. Since "听" refers to an action that is not realized yet, answer B should be ruled out. The difference between "也" and "又" is that "也" indicates the similarity of the actions or states, which could either be one that have happened or one that are to happen, meaning that the same action or state has happened or will happen to a different object. So when "也" is used, there should be a comparable item. As for "又", the action must be a thing to happen, and there is no comparable item. The difference between "再" and "还" lies in that "还" should be put before a modal verb, while "再" should be put before the main verb. According to the meaning and the syntactic structure, answer A should be chosen.

144. The correct answer is D.

"再", "又", "还" and "也" are all relative adverbs that can be used to indicate the repeat, recurrence or continuity of an action or behaviour. When indicating a recurrent or continuous action, both of "再" and "还" refer to an action to be realized, and "又" expresses actions that have already come true. The difference between "也" and "又" is that "也" indicates similarity, meaning that the same action or state has happened to a different object. So when "也" is used, there should be a comparable item.

"又" indicates repeat and recurrence, meaning that the same kind of action or behaviour has happened to the same object. In this sentence, "他" is the comparable item of "你". The two parts before and after the relative elements have similar nature. So "也" should be chosen here as the right relative word.

145. The correct answer is C.

"再", "又", "还" and "也" are all relative adverbs that can be used to indicate the repeat, recurrence or continuity of an action or behaviour. When indicating a recurrent or continuous action, both of "再" and "还" refer to actions to be realized, and "又" expresses actions that have already come true. The difference between "也" and "又" is that "也" indicates similarity, meaning that the same action or state has happened to a different object. So when "也" is used, there should be a comparable item. "又" indicates repeat and recurrence, meaning that the same kind of action or behaviour has happened to the same object. Furthermore, "还" still has another usage, that is, it indicates the continuity of the same action or state, having the meaning of "仍旧(still)" and "依然(as before)". None of the three relative words have such a usage. So according to the meaning of the sentence, answer C should be chosen as the correct one.

## Prepositions

146. The correct answer is A.

"跟" is a preposition used to form prepositional structures with the noun element that follows it to function as an adverbial. Prepositional structures are usually put before the verbal structure. So both B and C should be ruled out. "一起" is an adverb functioning as an adverbial, and it should also be put before the verbal structure. So answer D should be ruled out, too.

147. The correct answer is C.

"从" is a preposition, and it constitutes a prepositional structure together with the noun elements that follow it to function as an adverbial. So both A and D should be ruled out. The position of the prepositional structure lies before the verbal structure. So answer B should be ruled out, too. Thus only C is correct.

148. The correct answer is D.

"当", "在", "离", and "从" are all prepositions, among which "在", "离" and "从" can combine with noun elements that are related to time or space positions to indicate position and direction, space scope, time point or period of time. When "当" indicates time, the noun elements that follow it should be points of time. For example, "当我看见他的时候,他正在买车票。(When I saw him, he was buying tickets.)" The phrase "朋友那儿" indicates the space position. So the preposition "当" can be ruled out. "在" indicates the point of the space position or the scope of the space. "离" indicates the distance between the two points. "从" can either refer to the starting point in terms of the time or that of the space. When it indicates the starting point of the space, it is usually followed by words with the reference of position or direction. According to the meaning of the sentence, "从" should be chosen.

149. The correct answer is C.

There are two explanations for this question. The first explanation is: if there is more than one adverbial in a sentence, their order in the Chinese language is (1) the adverbial indicating the time + (2) the adverbial indicating the tone or the relative relationship + (3) the adverbial describing the person who takes the action + (4) the adverbial indicating the aim, basis, relationship, and coordination + (5) the adverbial indicating the position, space, direction, and line + (6) the adverbial indicating the object + (7) the adverbial describing the action. "七点钟" is a time adverbial, and the phrase "从家" is an adverbial indicating the place and direction. Their order should be that the time adverbial comes first. So answer C should be chosen. The second explanation is: time words are nominal. They can perform the role of the object or the subject of a sentence while prepositional structures can only be the adverbial or complement of a sentence. The prepositional structure introduced by "从" can only be the adverbial of a sentence. Generally speaking, the subject is at the head of a sentence, and adverbials are usually before the verb. So the sentence "他每天七点钟从家去学校" actually has a triple-subject: "他", "每天", and "七点钟", which are the triple topic of the sentence.

150. The correct answer is B.

The preposition "从", combined with nouns indicating the place or time, could indicates the starting point of an action or time, and in this situation, there should be such words indicating directions, as "到", "去", "向", "朝", and "往", etc., to correspond with it. Sometimes, it can also be combined with place nouns to indicate the place of passage. In this situation, the verbs are usually "经过" and "路过", etc. This question does not meet those requirements. So answer A could be ruled out. "在" indicates the place where an action happens or a thing exists. "往" and "向" indicate the direction of an action or behaviour. "散步" is a verb that has no direction, and so it cannot be combined with "往" and "向", both of which indicate the direction. In this way, both of answers C and D can be ruled out.

151. The correct answer is A.

Both of "向" and "往" can indicate the direction of a behaviour or an action. But the nominal element behind "向" can either be an object or a nominal element indicating a place or direction while the nominal element after "往" can only be one indicating a place or direction, but not an object. "我" is not the noun indicating place and direction, but an object. So only "向" can be chosen. "从", combined with a noun of place or time, indicates the starting point of an action or behaviour or the starting point of time, and in this situation, it is generally followed by words indicating the direction, such as "到", "去", "向", "朝" and "往" etc., to correspond with it. Sometimes it can also be combined with place nouns to indicate the place of passage. And the verbs used together are usually "经过" and "路过", etc. This sentence does not meet those requirements. So answer B can be ruled out. "在" indicates the place where an action happens or a thing exists, and behind it, there should be nominal elements indicating the place and direction. "我" does not have such a meaning. So answer D should be ruled out.

152. The correct answer is C.

"往", "在", "朝" and "从" are all prepositions that are related to the place or direction. Among them, "往" and "朝" are directional, while "在" and "从" have no such a meaning. "朝" indicates the direction one faces and "往" indicates the direction in which the behaviour or act goes, and the nominal elements following them can only be one indicating place or direction. "从", combined with a noun indicating place or time, refers to the starting point of an action or time, and in this situation, there are usually words indicating directions, such as "到", "去", "向", "朝" and "往", etc., to correspond with it. Sometimes, it can also be combined with place nouns, indicating the place of passage. At this time, the verbs used together are usually "经过" and "路过", etc. "阳", the shorten word of "太阳", means the direction something faces. So the preposition "朝" should be chosen.

153. The correct answer is D.

"从", combined with a noun indicating place or time, refers to the starting point of an action or time, and at this time, there are usually such words that indicate directions, as "到", "去", "向", "朝" and "往", to correspond with it. Sometimes, it can also be combined with place nouns, indicating the place of passage. At this time, the verbs concerned are usually "经过" and "路过", etc. Both "向" and "往" can indicate the direction of a behaviour or an action. But the nominal element behind "向" can be either an object or a nominal element having the characteristics of a place or direction while the nominal element after "往" can only be one having the characteristics of a place or direction, but not an object. "离" indicates the distance between the two points (in space or time), and there should be a measure word indicating distance to be used after it. This sentence just meets this requirement. So answer D should be chosen as the correct one.

154. The correct answer is A.

"从", combined with a noun indicating place or time, refers to the starting point of an action or time, and at this time, there are usually such words that indicate directions as "到", "去", "向", "朝" and "往", to correspond with it. This sentence just meets the two conditions of having a time word and the verb "到". So "从" should be chosen. "离" indicates the distance between the two points (in space or time), and there should be a measure word indicating distance to be used behind it. "在" indicates the place where an action happens or a thing exists. What are followed should be nominal elements indicating place and direction. "当" indicates the time point. So none of answers B, C and D are suitable.

155. The correct answer is A.

What follows "当" should be words indicating time. "太阳升起的时候" is just such a phrase indicating the time. So answer A should be chosen. What follows "朝" should be words indicating the direction, for example: "朝南", "朝北", and "朝太阳升起的地方". What follows "向" should also be words indicating the direction, for example: "向南", "向北" and "向太阳升起的地方". What follows "离" should be words indicating place, and there should also be a measure word indicating distance or such adjectives as "远" or "近".

156. The correct answer is B.

As a preposition, "对" can be used to introduce the object of an action or someone that has some relation with the action, for example, "他". Under this condition, only A and B meet the requirement. In the combination of "对 + NP + VP", if VP is a verb or a verbal phrase, the negative word "不" should be put before "对", for example, "不对他负责", "不对他发脾气"; if VP is an adjective or an adjective phrase, the negative word "不" should be put before the adjective or the adjective phrase, for example, "对他不好" and "对我不怎么热情". So answer B should be chosen as the correct one.

157. The correct answer is C.

The three prepositions "对于", "关于" and "对" can all introduce after them the object of the action or something that has some relation with the action. But "对于" and "关于" can only be used at the head of the sentence, and they cannot be used in the middle of the sentence. For example, we can say "对于这件事我们要进行调查", or "关于这件事我们要进行调查", but not "我们要对于/关于这件事进行调查". Whereas the preposition "对", after forming a prepositional structure, can either be put at the head of the sentence or in the middle of the sentence. Taking this question as an example, we can say "我们要对这件事进行调查", "我们对这件事要进行调查" or "对这件事我们要进行调查". "有关" is a verb and is generally used together with the preposition "与" to constitute the structure "与……有关". For example, "空气不好与汽车尾气有关".

158. The correct answer is A.

"为" is a preposition. It could be used together with the noun or the nominal words to constitute a prepositional structure, which can only be put before the predicative word functioning as an adverbial. In this sentence, "作报告" is a predicative phrase. And it is only in answer A that the prepositional phrase "为我们" is put before the predicative word. So A should be chosen as the correct one.

159. The correct answer is A.

"给" is a preposition. It could be used with the noun or the nominal words or phrases to constitute a prepositional structure to function either as an adverbial in front of the verbal words, for example, "给我买礼物"; or as a complement after the verbal phrase, for example, "扔给我一件衣服". What is more, "给" can also be used in a sentence as a mark of the passive voice, for example, "把自己给锁在外边了". In addition, "给" can be used as a verb and appears in the structure of double objects, for example, "给我一件礼物"; or appears in the structure of consecutive predicates, for example, "买一件礼物给我". Here in this question, "给" is a preposition. And only answer C can meet the requirement of the prepositional structure that is used as an adverbial.

160. The correct answer is D.

"跟" is a preposition that can be used together with the noun or the nominal words or phrases to constitute a prepositional structure and function as an adverbial before the verbal phrase. The prepositional structure composed by "跟" cannot be used as a complement and so it can not appear after the verbal structure. In this way, answers B and C can both be ruled out. If there is more than one adverbial, the prepositional structure should be put in the front. So we should choose "跟新郎一起度蜜月" and rule out "一起跟新郎度蜜月".

161. The correct answer is C.

The sentence with "比" is formed like this: "NP$_1$ + 比 + NP$_2$ + VP", in which the two compared items are connected by "比". The VP, used as the predicate, can be an adjective, adjective phrase or verbal phrase, for example, "这座山比那座山高", "这座山比那座山高多了" and "他比我更有资格当总理". The prepositional structure constituted by "比" cannot be used as a complement, and so "NP$_2$" cannot appear after the verbal phrase. In this way, answer A can be ruled out. What is more, "比" can neither be used alone before the predicative elements or at the end of a sentence to function as a grammatical element. In this way, answers B and D can be ruled out, and C should be chosen as the correct one.

162. The correct answer is A.

"为", as a preposition, can be used to introduce the beneficiaries of the action or behavior to form a prepositional phrase; while "为了", as a conjunction, can be used to introduce the adverbial clause indicating the aim or purpose. "因为" is also a conjunction, but used to introduce a clause indicating the reason. "祖国贡献力量" cannot stand alone as a sentence, and so it is not a clause. In this way, both answers B and C can be ruled out. "作为" in answer D is a verb, and can only be followed by nominal elements. So answer D can also be ruled out. Only the preposition "为" in answer A, with the noun "祖国", could form a prepositional phrase modifying the verbal structure "贡献力量". So only answer A could be chosen as the correct one.

163. The correct answer is A.

In the sentences with the character "把", the negative adverb should be put before the preposition "把". In this way, answers B and D could be ruled our. In a "把" sentence, if the predicative element after "把" is not composed by "一 + V", there should be some elements used as the complement or the aspect marker "了" after the verb, otherwise, the sentence is not acceptable in terms of structure. In this way, answer C can also be ruled out.

164. The correct answer is C.

In Chinese, the passive sentence can be composed by the preposional structures introduced by "被", "叫" or "让". But there are some preconditions for a passive sentence to stand as that. In such passive structures as "X 被 Y + VP", the structure can stand only when X is the typical patient of Y in semantic terms. For example, in the sentence "他的作业本被他弄丢了", the nominal phrase "他的作业本" is the typical patient of the VP "弄丢了". In the sentence "他的数学作业被他做得一塌糊涂", "他的数学作业" is the typical patient of the VP "做得一塌糊涂". If the element at the position of X is only an ordinary topic, it is not so necessary to use a passive sentence in Chinese. So answer C should be chosen as the correct one.

165. The correct answer is D.

In the Chinese language, the passive sentence can be marked by "被", "叫", "让" and "给". When "叫" or "让" is used, the agent must appear, for example, "照相机叫孩子弄坏了", or "照相机让孩子弄坏了". When "被" is used, there is no such restriction. The doer can appear or does not appear. "把" is a preposition indicating the meaning of causing something to be done, and in a passive sentence, it must be used together with "给". For example, "孩子把照相机给弄坏了".

Conjunctions

166. The correct answer is B.

Both of "或者" and "还是" are conjunctions indicating the selective relationship, but they are quite different. "或者" means to select from two or more than two possibilities or choices that are offered. It cannot be used in interrogative sentences. "还是" could only be used in interrogative sentences, asking about which one to choose from the two or more than two possibilities or objects that are given. What should be noted is that, if the sentence, in which "还是" is used, is an element contained in a bigger sentence, it may not indicate questioning. For example: (1) the clause in which "还是" is used is the object of the verb that precedes, for instance, "我真的不知道你是中国人还是日本人"; (2) the sub-sentence that contains "还是" is used in the front, and is followed by a clause to summarize and assess, for instance, "他今天晚上去看电影还是听音乐会,我不知道". What "和" and "跟" connect are substantival elements, and they could not be used to indicate the selective relationship, and thus they should be ruled out.

167. The correct answer is C.

"为了" is a conjunction used to introduce a clause indicating the purpose. "虽然" is a conjunction that links a transitional clause. "因为" is a conjunction that links a reason clause. According to the meaning of the sentence, this is a compound sentence indicating the cause and the result. And what is needed here should be a conjunction indicating the relationship of the cause and result. So answer C should be chosen. "原因" is a noun, and should be ruled out.

168. The correct answer is C.

Both of "还是" and "或者" are conjunctions indicating the selective relationship, but they are quite different. "或者" means to select from two or more than two possibilities or objects that are offered, and it cannot be used in interrogative sentences. "还是" could only be used in interrogative sentences, asking about which one to choose from two or more than two possibilities or objects that are given. What should be noted is that, if the sentence in which "还是" is used is an element contained in a bigger sentence, it may not indicate questioning. For example: "我真的不知道你是中国人还是日本人" and "他今天晚上去看电影还是听音乐会，我不知道". Here is a narrative sentence and it is not a sub-sentence contained in a bigger one. So "还是" should be ruled out. "并且" and "而且" are used to connect two predicative elements, indicating that the latter part is more strong in terms of the tone or meaning. Here in this sentence, both "小张" and "小王" are substantival elements. So they should not be chosen.

169. The correct answer is A.

Both of "和" and "跟" are conjunctions indicating the coordinate relationship. The two parts linked by them are substantival. "很大" and "很漂亮" are both predicative, and so answers B and C can be ruled out. "虽然" is a conjunction indicating the turning of the tone, and it is usually used together with the conjunction "但是". The two predicative elements linked by this pair of conjunctions are contrary or opposed to each other in semantic meaning. Thus it can also be ruled out. "而且" is a conjunction indicating the increase by degrees, which can be used to link up two predicative elements, expressing the progressiveness of meaning. So answer A should be chosen as the correct one.

Auxiliary Words

170. The correct answer is C.

The auxiliary "的" could be used after a verb to indicate the dynamic state, but the topic of the sentence must be the object that the speaker would like to emphasize. For example: in the sentence "是我去的上海", the verb "是" is used to emphasize the topic "我"; in "我上星期天去的上海", the topic "上星期天" is emphasized by being stressed, and in "我坐飞机去的上海", "坐飞机" is emphasized by being stressed. According to the meaning of the sentence, there is nothing to be emphasized here. So "的" cannot be used here. "得" is a structural auxiliary, and it is often used in between the verb and its complement indicating the result or possibility, which should be predicative. "几个公园" in this sentence, however, are substantival, and should be the object of the verb. In this way, "得" can also be ruled out. "着" and "了" are dynamic auxiliaries with "了" indicating the realization of the action and "着" indicating the going on of an action. According to the meaning of the sentence, "去" is an action that was completed last Sunday. So answer C should be chosen.

171. The correct answer is C.

"了" is a dynamic auxiliary indicating the aspect of being realized (perfect). It cannot co-occur with "没有", that is to say, there is no such sentence as "没有……了". "着" is a dynamic auxiliary indicating the aspect of progressiveness and it cannot co-occur with "没有", either. "过" is a dynamic auxiliary indicating the voice of having experienced, meaning that something has been experienced. Its negative form is "没(有) + verb + 过". The structural auxiliary "得" is used in between a verb and a complement indicating the result or possibility, which should be predicative.

172. The correct answer is D.

"着" and "过" indicate the progressive and the perfect aspects respectively. "呢" is often used at the end of a narrative sentence, with such words as "正、正在、在(哪里)" and "着", to indicate the progressive or continous state of the action. "了" can be used either as a dynamic auxiliary or a modal particle, and is usually placed at the end of a sentence to indicate that some changes have happened.

173. The correct answer is C.

"过" is always used after a verb and before an object. Among the four answers, only A and C meet this requirement. Here in this sentence, "三次" is a numeral-classifier compound that is used as the attribute of the object "课", and should be put before it. So A is also wrong.

174. The correct answer is B.

"过", "了", "着" and "的" are all aspect markers, among which, "过" indicates "有过经历 (having experienced)", "了" indicates "实现某种变化 (some changes have taken place)", "着" indicates "某种动作行为正在进行或持续 (a certain action or behaviour is going on or in progression)", and "的" indicates "对某一动作行为以及与该动作行为有关的论元的肯定 (the affirmation of a certain action or behaviour, or the elements concerning this action or behaviour)", and it could usually be changed into the structure of "是……的", in which the element after "是" is just the object being affirmed. "已经有不少进步" indicates "实现了某种变化 (some changes have taken place)" in terms of meaning. So "了" should be chosen.

175. The correct answer is A.

This is an imperative sentence, and so there should be an auxiliary at the end of the sentence indicating the imperative tone. In the standard Chinese language, the following modal particles are used to show the different tones: "吗", "啊", "吧", "呢", "了", "呕" and their various forms (for example, "呀", "哪", and "哇", etc. are all various forms of "啊"). Among them, the auxiliary indicating the imperative tone is "吧". So answer A is chosen as the correct one.

176. The correct answer is C.

Extent adverbs can be used together with adjectives to indicate the extent. Yet when they are used as such, they would appear either before the adjective or after the adjective, but not appear before and after the adjective at the same time. So both A and B can be ruled out. What is more, both "很" and "极" are extent adverbs and they cannot be used together to modify the ajective "漂亮". So D is also wrong.

177. The correct answer is A.

In Chinese putonghua, "多", as an adjective, could be used together with a verb and a measure word to form the structure of "多 + V + Numeral-classifier compound", meaning that the number has increased. In the structure, "多" is used as an adverbial. For example, "多买一瓶". In the Cantonese dialect, however, the pattern would be "V + 多 + Numeral-classifier compound". For example, "买多一瓶".

178. The correct answer is D.

The pattern "verb + 得 + complement" is the affirmative form of the complement indicating possibility, and its negative forms are as follows: "verb + 不 + complement" or "没(有) + verb + complement". So both of the affirmative form "买得到" and the negative form "买不到" are structures that can stand up in the view of grammar. According to the meaning of the sentence, the negative form should be adopted here. So only "买不到" in answer D is right here.

179. The correct answer is A.

Extent adverbs can be used together with adjectives to indicate the extent. But when they are used as such, they would appear either before the adjective or after it, but not appear before and after the adjective at the same time. So answer C can be ruled out. Both of "很" and "非常" are extent adverbs and they cannot be used together. So answer D is also wrong. What is more, in the structure "adjective + 得 + complement" indicating the degree, the extent adverb can only be placed after "得" to be the complement. So answer B is also wrong.

180. The correct answer is C.

A monosyllabic adjective, after being modified by the adv. "很", can no longer be used either as an adverbial or the complement of a bare verb. So both A and B cannot stand. Yet the reduplicated monosyllabic adjective can be used either as an adverbial, for example: "满满斟了一杯酒"; or as an attribute, for example: "满满一杯酒一口就喝干了"; or as a predicate or a complement after the auxilary "的" being added after, for example: "酒满满的", and "酒倒得满满的". Here in this sentence, there is no "的" after the reduplicated monosyllabic adjective "慢慢", and thus it can only be placed before a verb as an adverbial, but not a complement. So answer C should be chosen as the correct one.

181. The correct answer is A.

In Chinese putonghua, "多", as an adjective, could be used together with a verb and a measure word to form the structure of "多 + verb + measure word", meaning the number has increased, and in this situation, "多" is used as an adverbial. Only answer A meets the requirement of the combination order of this pattern. In the Cantonese dialect, however, the pattern is "verb + 多 + measure word".

182. The correct answer is C.

When using together with the verb and the adjective, the measure word "一点儿" can only be put after them, not before. In this way, answers A and B can be ruled out. Yet, sometimes we could see such a sentence as "天气有一点儿冷", in which "一点儿" is used after "有", that is to say, "一点儿" has combined closely with "有", and it has no direct structural relation with the adjective "冷". The pattern "verb / adjective + (一) + 点儿" expresses that the extent or the quantity increases or decreases slightly, in which the numeral word "一" can be omitted. This structure can be used as a subject or predicate, but not as an attribute. When it is used as an attribute, "的" must be added. So answer D can be ruled out. Here in this sentence, "天气冷一点儿" is a subject-predicate phrase, in which, "冷一点儿" is the predicate of "天气".

183. The correct answer is B.

This is a sentence in which a subject-predicate structure is used as the predicate. "很" is an extent adverb, and it can modify such adjectives as "漂亮", but not the nouns "眼睛". So answer D should be ruled out. Furthermore, "很", without being used together with "得", cannot be placed after a predicative word as the complement. In this way, answer C can be ruled out. In addition, without "的" being added behind, the adjective modified by "很" cannot modify a noun. So answer A is also wrong.

184. The correct answer is D.

"已经" is a time adverb indicating "经历过 (having experienced)" or "完结 (having completed)". It is usually put after the element of the subject and before that of the predicate. Here in this sentence, "看过了" is a predicative element. Only answer D fits the situation where "已经" appears. This is a sentence where a subject-predicate structure is used as the predicate.

185. The correct answer is A.

This is a sentence that contains manifold attributes. The order of the manifold attributes is as follows: (1) nouns or pronouns indicating the possessive relationship; (2) place words and time words; (3) numeral phrases; (4) subject-predicate phrases; (5) verbs (or verbal phrases), and prepositional phrases; (6) adjectives + "的"; (7) adjectives and describing nouns without "的". The order of attributes of this sentence is (3), (6), (7).

186. The correct answer is C.

"不 + 怎么 + verb / adjective" is a fixed collocation, in which "怎么", means (not) very, (not) too, indicating a certain extent, and is somewhat equivalent to "很", but with an understated tone. The role of "怎么" is to weaken the strength of "不" and soften the tone. For example, "不怎么好" is less affirmative than "不好".

187. The correct answer is D.

The pattern using the verb "给" is: V + 给 + indirect object (receiver) + direct object (the thing to be received). Only answer D meets this condition.

188. The correct answer is A.

"没有" is a negative adverb. When it is used in interrogative sentences, either of the two following patterns could be used: (1) "verb / adjective（了）+ 没有", which is used for raising questions only, not for speculation, and answer A meets this condition; (2) "没有 + verb / adjective + 吗", indicating doubt or surprise that need to be confirmed. The questioning form can be used as an element in a complex sentence, just as the case in this sentence. Furthermore, "没有" can not co-occur with "了" in the following condition: "没有 + verb / adjective + 了(le)". So both B and C should be ruled out.

189. The correct answer is D.

"不" is a negative adverb, and appears before a verb or adjective. In this way, answers A and C can be ruled out. "不 + adjective" can no longer be used to modify a nominal element. So answer B can also be ruled out.

190. The correct answer is B.

The situation where the directional verb "出" appears is as follows: "verb + 出 + noun (indicating place)" or "从 + noun (indicating place) + verb + complement (with "出")". Only answer B meets this condition.

191. The correct answer is A.

"adjective + 多 + 了" is a fixed collocation, which can be used to indicate: (1) the extent has increased, for example: "她的病好多了"; (2) there is some distance between the present condition and a certain reference standard, for example: "他的身高比要求矮多了".

192. The correct answer is B.

" adjective + 得 + 多" is a fixed collocation that is used in a comparative sentence, indicating the great difference in terms of the extent, for example: "好得多", "快得多", etc.

193. The correct answer is A.

If such verbs as "等" is followed by a numeral-classifier compound as its object, the object is usually a measure word indicating the time. "一点儿" is not a measure word indicating the time. So answers C and D should be ruled out. "一会儿" indicates that an action lasts very shortly, and it can only be used as an object behind "等", but not before it.

194. The correct answer is B.

The dynamic auxiliary "过", indicating the aspect of having experienced, appears exactly after a verb or a predicate-complement structure. In this way, only answers B and C meet the requirement. If it appears in a predicate-object structure, the position of "过"

lies in between the predicate and the object. When a numeral-classifier compound appears before a verb, it must be the negative structure and the numeral is limited only to "一", for example: "一遍也没看过". Answer C is not a negative structure, and the numeral is not "一", either. So it should be ruled out.

195. The correct answer is C.

"有" is a verb indicating ownership, possession or existence. If the subject of the sentence is a human being or an institution, "有" means owning, for example: "学校有很多汽车", which means "学校拥有很多汽车 (The school has many cars)". If the subject of the sentence is an abstract word, "有" means that it has got some kind of attribute or some result, for example: "他的汉语水平有进步 (His Chinese has been improved)". If the subject of the sentence is a word that indicates position or time, "有" means existence. The verb "有" in this sentence indicates existence, and in such a sentence, there is usually an object that exists and a place where the object exists, which constitutes the pattern of "the place where something exists + 有 + something that exists". Here, only answers C and D meet the requirement of this pattern. "很多汽车" is a nominal element and naturally, it can be used as the object of "有". "汽车很多" is a predicative element, and it is not acceptable to be the object of "有".

196. The correct answer is A.

"有" is a verb indicating owning, possession or existence. If the subject of the sentence is a human being or an institution, "有" means owning, for example: "学校有很多汽车", which means "学校拥有很多汽车". If the subject of the sentence is an abstract word, "有" means that it has got some kind of attribute or some result, for example: "他的汉语水平有进步". If the subject of the sentence is a word that indicates position or time, "有" means existence. Here in this sentence, "生活水平" is an abstract noun, and "有" indicates having got the result. "提高" is the object of "有", and "很大" is used as the attribute of "提高".

197. The correct answer is B.

In modern Chinese, if there are both an object and a complement in a sentence, their order of combination should be VCO (verb + complement + object), for example: "吃饱饭", whereas the order VOC (verb + object + complement) is not acceptable, for example: "吃饭饱". So answer A is unacceptable, and answer B is acceptable. If in a sentence, there are both a complement and an aspect marker, the aspect marker appears after the complement, for example: "VC 了", but not "V 了 C". So answer C is also wrong. When an adjective and a verb co-occur in a sentence, except in very rare cases, the adjective always appears after the verb to function as its complement. It is very rare to see that an adjective is used before a verb to function as an adverbial. So answer D can also be ruled out.

198. The correct answer is D.

"小孩儿" is a nominal element. What lies before it can either be a transitive verb or an adjective or a numeral-classifier compound. Here in this sentence, there is only one intransitive verb "跑", which cannot appear before "小孩儿". The only one that can appear before it is answer D.

199. The correct answer is B.

"学生" is a nominal element. What lies before it can either be a transitive verb or an adjective or a measure word. Here in this sentence, there is only one intransitive verb "死", which cannot appear before "学生". The only one that can appear before it is answer B.

200. The correct answer is C.

This is a rhetoric question, whose pattern is "不是……吗". If there is an adverb, it should appear before "是". It is affirmative in meaning with an obvious tone of "事实如此 (it is just the fact!)". "就不是" indicates negative. "不是就" and "就是不" should have a predicative structure after them. In this way, all the three choices should be ruled out.

# 中国汉语水平考试语法结构
## （初、中等）模拟练习

## 第1套

### 二、语法结构
（30题，20分钟）

#### 第一部分

说明：51~60题，在每一个句子下面都有一个指定词语，句中 A B C D 是供选择的四个不同位置，请判断这一词语放在句子中哪个位置上恰当。

例如：

　　55. 我们A一起B去上海C旅游D过。

　　　　　没有

"没有"只有放在 A 的位置上，使全句变为"我们没有一起去上海旅游过"，才合乎语法。所以第55题惟一恰当的答案是 A，你应在答卷上找到号码55，在字母 A 上画一横道，横道一定要画得粗一些，重一些。

　　55. [★]　[B]　[C]　[D]

51. 我们 A 先商量 B 商量，等他 C 回来就把结果 D 告诉他。

　　　　　　　　一

52. A 再 B 到 C 去 D 的时候，我一定见见你父母。

　　　　　　　上海

53. 他是 A 我们学校 B 去年评选出的 C 学生 D 干部。

　　　　　　　　优秀

54. 今天我打算 A 买 B 自行车 C 再去 D 逛商场。

　　　　　　　先

55. 你买的那个花瓶 A 已经 B 打碎 C 了 D。

　　　　　　　被他

56. 大家 A 一致要求 B 他说 C 他跟小李恋爱 D 的经过。

　　　　　　　一遍

57. 西单商场 A 的东西 B 可能 C 贵 D。

　　　　　　　有些

58. 吃烤鸭的时候,先A把鸭片放B在饼里,然后把葱丝C蘸一下再D卷在饼里。

在酱里

59. 重要的不是A读了多少书,而是B把C读过的东西运用D到实践中去。

如何

60. A到中国B来以后,我C在冬天去哈尔滨旅行D过一次。

曾

## 第二部分

说明:61~80题,每个句子中有一个或两个空儿,请在A B C D四个答案中选择惟一恰当的填上(在答卷上的字母上画一横道)。

例如:

67. 我昨天买了一____钢笔。

  A.件  B.块  C.枝  D.条

我们只能说"我昨天买了一枝钢笔",所以第67题惟一恰当的答案是C,你应在答卷上找到号码67,在字母C上画一横道,横道一定要画得粗一些,重一些。

67. [A] [B] [C] [D]

61. 透过两____玻璃窗,我们可以看见绿色的田野。
  A.面    B.张
  C.片    D.扇

62. 夜里,他剧烈地咳嗽了____,喝了点热水才渐渐平息下去。
  A.一趟    B.一阵
  C.一顿    D.一些

63. 在我的记忆____,她是一个非常美丽非常善良的人。
  A.中    B.内
  C.上    D.着

64. 听说儿子考上了大学,他乐得嘴都合不____了。
  A.下    B.起
  C.上    D.着

65. 她____怎样教育孩子一点也不关心。
  A.至于    B.对于
  C.就    D.向

66. 他____怎样学好汉语发表了一点看法。
  A.向    B.从
  C.至于    D.就

67. 让他讲____,有什么问题等他讲完以后再说。

A. 起来　　　　B. 下去
C. 下来　　　　D. 过去

68. 我们经常一起去看电影____听音乐会。
    A. 还要　　　　B. 或者
    C. 或许　　　　D. 还是

69. 父亲去世的消息对她来说太____了。
    A. 忽然　　　　B. 居然
    C. 突然　　　　D. 果然

70. ____明天不下雨,我们就去郊游。
    A. 即使　　　　B. 如果
    C. 就算　　　　D. 虽然

71. 早睡早起,注意饮食,____一个人的健康十分重要。
    A. 对　　　　　B. 关于
    C. 使　　　　　D. 为

72. 他们是离婚了,但____曾在一起生活过十几年,偶而见上一面也是可以理解的。
    A. 根据　　　　B. 毕竟
    C. 甚至　　　　D. 如何

73. 他给我讲了好几遍,____使我明白了其中的含义。
    A. 好让　　　　B. 故意
    C. 只好　　　　D. 终于

74. 他____做什么事都那么认真。
    A. 无论　　　　B. 即使
    C. 假如　　　　D. 只管

75. 刚从地平线上升起的太阳____。
    A. 通通红的
    B. 通红红的
    C. 通通红红的
    D. 通红通红的

76. 这件事得____。
    A. 你们自己去办才行
    B. 自己你们去办才行
    C. 去办你们自己才行
    D. 去办自己你们才行

77. 这是一个____!
    A. 令人兴奋多么的消息啊
    B. 兴奋的消息多么令人吧
    C. 令人多么兴奋的消息吧
    D. 多么令人兴奋的消息啊

78. 请你一定____。
    A. 把这封信交给他亲手
    B. 把交给他这封信亲手
    C. 把这封信亲手交给他
    D. 这封信把亲手交给他

79. 我们的老师就在那边,这个问题你去跟他____吧。
    A. 谈谈了　　　B. 谈一谈
    C. 谈了谈　　　D. 谈了谈了

80. 房上、树上、地上都____。
    A. 盖了一层的白雪厚厚
    B. 盖了厚厚的白雪一层
    C. 厚厚的白雪一层盖了
    D. 盖了一层厚厚的白雪

## 第2套

### 二、语法结构
（30题，20分钟）

#### 第一部分

说明：51～60题，在每一个句子下面都有一个指定词语，句中ＡＢＣＤ是供选择的四个不同位置，请判断这一词语放在句子中哪个位置上恰当。

例如：

　　55. 我们 A 一起 B 去上海 C 旅游 D 过。
　　　　　　　没有

"没有"只有放在 A 的位置上，使全句变为"我们没有一起去上海旅游过"，才合乎语法。所以第 55 题惟一恰当的答案是 A，你应在答卷上找到号码55，在字母 A 上画一横道，横道一定要画得粗一些，重一些。

　　55. [★]　　[B]　　[C]　　[D]

51. 他吃完 A 早饭，背 B 起书包，踏 C 上自行车，向学校骑 D 去。
　　　　　　　了

52. 学生们来得 A 很早，在会议 B 以前 C 就 D 都坐好了。
　　　　　　　开始

53. 她正跳 A 舞，忽然发现 B 他站 C 在角落里 D 静静看着她。
　　　　　　　着

54. A 他们家 B 搬走 C 了一个月 D 了。
　　　　　　　已经

55. 昨天刚 A 从商店买 B 来的 C 新袜子 D 放在哪了？
　　　　　　　几双

56. 现在我只 A 想跟他 B 浪漫，C 将来是否结婚 D 我根本不在乎。
　　　　　　　至于

57. 那个电影 A 我 B 看了一遍 C 可 D 还是不完全明白。
　　　　　　　又

58. 爸爸 A 很快会 B 给我们一笔钱，C 让我们早日 D 出国留学。
　　　　　　　好

59. 现在 A 请你 B 讲一讲 C 你从一个下岗工人 D 变成一个企业家的经过。
　　　　　　　给大家

60. 她 A 的歌声 B 吸引 C 住了我 D。
　　　　　　　一下子

## 第二部分

说明:61~80题,每个句子中有一个或两个空儿,请在 A、B、C、D 四个答案中选择惟一恰当的填上(在答卷上的字母上画一横道)。

例如:
67. 我昨天买了一____钢笔。
 A. 件　　B. 块　　C. 枝　　D. 条

我们只能说"我昨天买了一枝钢笔",所以第67题惟一恰当的答案是 C,你应在答卷上找到号码67,在字母 C 上画一横道,横道一定要画得粗一些,重一些。

67. [A]　[B]　[⊂]　[D]

---

61. 他非常喜欢文学,从十几岁起____写诗,写散文,也写小说。
 A. 才　　　　B. 就
 C. 又　　　　D. 再

62. 关于如何学好汉语,我们的看法有____的地方。
 A. 一致　　　B. 一起
 C. 一概　　　D. 一律

63. 在中国文学史____有个名叫李白的大诗人。
 A. 里　　　　B. 内
 C. 上　　　　D. 下

64. 作为一名小学老师,她有一____火热的爱心。
 A. 个　　　　B. 腔
 C. 棵　　　　D. 颗

65. 请代我____你爸爸妈妈问好。
 A. 为　　　　B. 致
 C. 向　　　　D. 把

66. 听说下周____要派你去广州出差。
 A. 将会　　　B. 可能
 C. 可以　　　D. 能够

67. 这块玻璃____是他打碎的,可他却不承认。
 A. 明明　　　B. 明白
 C. 明朗　　　D. 清楚

68. 我知道他是这儿的学生,____具体在哪个班我就不清楚了。
 A. 虽然　　　B. 只有
 C. 不过　　　D. 假如

69. 这件事情看____还真有点麻烦,我们不如找他商量一下再说吧。
 A. 过来　　　B. 上来
 C. 下来　　　D. 起来

70. 这家商店是专卖____用品的。
 A. 经常　　　B. 平常
 C. 通常　　　D. 日常

71. 对上周发生的那件事我没____可说的。

A. 多么 B. 怎么
C. 什么 D. 那么

72. ____ 男孩女孩，____ 享有同等受教育的权力。
    A. 无论……都  B. 既然……就
    C. 虽然……但  D. 不管……也

73. ____ 她不同意，你 ____ 再去找别人。
    A. 只有……就  B. 尽管……才
    C. 如果……就  D. 既然……也

74. 他昨天晚上上 ____ 火车。
    A. 了  B. 的
    C. 过  D. 看

75. 中午男朋友要来看她，一大早她就打扮得 _____ 的。
    A. 漂漂亮亮
    B. 漂亮漂亮
    C. 漂一漂亮
    D. 漂亮了漂亮

76. 他就住在附近，要不你就 _____。
    A. 找他去到他家
    B. 到他家找他去

C. 他到家去找他
D. 找他到他家去

77. 昨天晚上作业太多了，我 _____。
    A. 只睡了三个小时觉
    B. 只三个小时睡觉
    C. 三个小时只睡觉
    D. 只睡觉了三个小时

78. 我不知道 _____。
    A. 谁是作者那本书的
    B. 作者那本书的是谁
    C. 是谁那本书的作者
    D. 那本书的作者是谁

79. 大家 _____ 地讨论起来了。
    A. 你一言我一语
    B. 一你言一我语
    C. 我一语你一言
    D. 你言一我语一

80. _____，我们一起去长城。
    A. 九点明天大家都到这儿来
    B. 大家都到明天九点这儿来
    C. 大家九点明天都到这儿来
    D. 明天九点大家都到这儿来

## 第3套

### 二、语法结构

（30题，20分钟）

#### 第一部分

说明：51～60题，在每一个句子下面都有一个指定词语，句中 A B C D 是供选择的四个不同位置，请判断这一词语放在句子中哪个位置上恰当。

例如：

    55. 我们 A 一起 B 去上海 C 旅游 D 过。

              没有

"没有"只有放在 A 的位置上，使全句变为"我们没有一起去上海旅游过"，才合乎语法。所以第 55 题惟一恰当的答案是 A，你应在答卷上找到号码 55，在字母 A 上画一横道，横道一定要画得粗一些，重一些。

    55. [★]  [B]  [C]  [D]

51. 我以前 A 曾去 B 过 C 香山，这回不想 D 再去了。

         三次

52. A 天 B 蒙蒙亮，我 C 就听见走廊里 D 有很多脚步声。

         刚

53. 爬到 A 山顶 B 的时候，C 我感觉 D 累极了。

         真是

54. 他看上去 A 也就 B 二十 C 岁 D。

         多

55. A 他 B 那 C 白色 D 衬衫的扣子都不全了。

         两件

56. 屋里烟太浓了，A 快 B 到 C 去 D 吧。

         外面

57. 跟妈妈在一起 A 住久了，B 舍不得 C 离开 D。

         真有点

58. A 我们 B 一起 C 去海边玩儿过 D。

         从未

59. 你 A 到桌子 B 去看看 C 有没有 D 报纸。

         那儿

60. 去年他生病 A 都 B 是他 C 姐姐照顾 D 他。

         那会儿

## 第二部分

说明:61~80题,每个句子中有一个或两个空儿,请在 A B C D 四个答案中选择惟一恰当的填上(在答卷上的字母上画一横道)。

例如:

　　67. 我昨天买了一____钢笔。

　　　　A. 件　　B. 块　　C. 枝　　D. 条

我们只能说"我昨天买了一枝钢笔",所以第67题惟一恰当的答案是C,你应在答卷上找到号码67,在字母C上画一横道,横道一定要画得粗一些,重一些。

　　67. [A]　[B]　[C]　[D]

61. 昨天《北京晚报》上报导了一____惊人的消息。
    A. 份　　　　　　B. 篇
    C. 页　　　　　　D. 则

62. 我 ____ 他只有一面之交,但却终生难忘。
    A. 对　　　　　　B. 跟
    C. 为　　　　　　D. 连

63. 他在各个方面都 ____ 自己要求十分严格。
    A. 从　　　　　　B. 与
    C. 对　　　　　　D. 被

64. 启发式教学法被各大、中、小学广泛 ____ 。
    A. 采用　　　　　B. 通用
    C. 作用　　　　　D. 实用

65. 他的天赋很好,无论弹琴 ____ 绘画都比较擅长。
    A. 或者　　　　　B. 还是
    C. 还有　　　　　D. 或许

66. 从他的眼神里,我看____他十分恐惧。
    A. 出来　　　　　B. 上来
    C. 起来　　　　　D. 下来

67. 许多年过去了,老人的心愿还是没 ____ 实现。
    A. 要　　　　　　B. 想要
    C. 一定会　　　　D. 能

68. 我告诉过你多少遍了,可你 ____ 是不听。
    A. 再　　　　　　B. 就
    C. 也　　　　　　D. 又

69. 我就多出一张电影票,是给你 ____ 还是给他?
    A. 吗　　　　　　B. 吧
    C. 啦　　　　　　D. 呢

70. 再完美的人 ____ 难免有缺点。
    A. 也　　　　　　B. 还
    C. 就　　　　　　D. 却

71. 如果你真心承认错误,就应该 ____ 她道歉。
    A. 为　　　　　　B. 叫

模拟练习·第3套　109

C. 会 　　　　　D. 向

72. 在与他交往的过程 ____ 发生过许多不愉快的事。
    A. 里　　　　B. 上
    C. 中　　　　D. 内

73. ____ 她同意，这件事才能办成。
    A. 即使　　　B. 既然
    C. 如果　　　D. 只有

74. 很多人 _____ 就步入了社会。
    A. 一上中学完
    B. 一中学上完
    C. 上中学一完
    D. 一上完中学

75. 他这人就这样，无论学什么都 _____ 。
    A. 坚持下去不
    B. 不下去坚持
    C. 坚持不下去
    D. 坚不下去持

76. 如果你有时间，就把你的房间 _____ 。
    A. 整整理理
    B. 整理整理
    C. 整理一理
    D. 整了整理

77. 我 _____ 什么罪都受过，困难挫折多一些有什么了不起的？
    A. 苦什么都吃过
    B. 都吃过什么苦
    C. 都什么吃过苦
    D. 什么苦都吃过

78. 他别的没说，_____ 。
    A. 只说了那么一句话
    B. 只那么一句说了话
    C. 那么只一句说了话
    D. 那么一句话只说了

79. 他整天 _____ 。
    A. 在桌子上趴写个没完
    B. 写个没完在桌子上趴
    C. 趴在桌子上写个没完
    D. 在桌子上趴写没个完

80. 你估计 _____ ？
    A. 参加游行昨天的有多少人
    B. 昨天参加游行的有多少人
    C. 有多少人游行参加昨天
    D. 游行多少人参加昨天

# 第4套

## 二、语法结构
（30题，20分钟）

### 第一部分

说明：51~60题，在每一个句子下面都有一个指定词语，句中A B C D是供选择的四个不同位置，请判断这一词语放在句子中哪个位置上恰当。

例如：

　　55．我们 A 一起 B 去上海 C 旅游 D 过。

　　　　　没有

"没有"只有放在A的位置上，使全句变为"我们没有一起去上海旅游过"，才合乎语法。所以第55题惟一恰当的答案是A，你应在答卷上找到号码55，在字母A上画一横道，横道一定要画得粗一些，重一些。

　　55．[★]　[B]　[C]　[D]

---

51．那 A 是 B 因为 C 中药产生了 D 作用。

　　　　　　　也许

52．你 A 应该先 B 完成 C 然后再 D 看电视。

　　　　　　把作业

53．她 A 看了 B 不知 C 写来的 D 一封信，就哭了。

　　　　　　　谁

54．我现在的学习 A 比以前 B 紧，所以 C 有时间 D 看小说。

　　　　　　　不

55．我买了 A 很多 B 商务印书馆 C 出版的 D 书。

　　　　　关于语言学的

56．他 A 喜欢 B 活动，整天 C 呆在家里 D。

　　　　　不怎么

57．多劳多得 A，你比别人 B 多拿一百元 C 不好意思 D 的。

　　　　　没什么

58．他 A 学习数学、B 语文等，还要 C 学习音乐和绘画 D。

　　　　　除了

59．A 事情 B 只能 C 办，不能 D 着急。

　　　　一件一件

60．昨天 A 夜里 B 我做了一个 C 梦 D。

　　　　奇怪的

## 第二部分

说明:61~80题,每个句子中有一个或两个空儿,请在 A、B、C、D 四个答案中选择唯一恰当的填上(在答卷上的字母上画一横道)。

例如:
  67. 我昨天买了一____钢笔。
    A. 件  B. 块  C. 枝  D. 条

我们只能说"我昨天买了一枝钢笔",所以第 67 题惟一恰当的答案是 C,你应在答卷上找到号码 67,在字母 C 上画一横道,横道一定要画得粗一些,重一些。
  67. [A] [B] [C̶] [D]

61. 每年过春节,爸爸总要在门上贴____春联。
  A. 一双  B. 一副
  C. 一套  D. 一群

62. 这件事我办不了,所以还得请你跑____。
  A. 一遍  B. 一场
  C. 一顿  D. 一趟

63. 结婚以后他们很____。
  A. 恩爱  B. 恩情
  C. 爱情  D. 情爱

64. 他把那张画挂在屋子的____了。
  A. 墙里  B. 墙面
  C. 墙上  D. 墙中

65. 从前有一____姓姜。
  A. 家里  B. 家中
  C. 家门  D. 家

66. 我们只谈了____小时。
  A. 半一个  B. 一半个
  C. 一半  D. 半个

67. 特别是____毕业的大学生,失业可是个大问题。
  A. 刚才  B. 刚就
  C. 刚  D. 还

68. 去年我还是学生,____我是老师了。
  A. 现年  B. 今年
  C. 这年  D. 本年

69. ____对这件事表现了极大的兴趣和热情。
  A. 人群们  B. 人民们
  C. 人们  D. 公众们

70. 打____以后,他天天坚持听汉语广播。
  A. 这么  B. 这里
  C. 这些  D. 这儿

71. 成年人都很难忍受这种病痛的折磨,____他还是个孩子。
  A. 再说  B. 何况
  C. 难道  D. 而且

72. 应当____指出的是,持有这种偏见的人并非少数。

A. 特定　　　B. 特殊
C. 特别　　　D. 故意

73. 你刚跟他认识三个月，就把一切都给了他，____ 他是个骗子呢？
    A. 但是　　　B. 就算
    C. 即使　　　D. 万一

74. ____ 脑子有毛病，____ 谁也不会干那种蠢事。
    A. 如果……就
    B. 与其……不如
    C. 既然……就
    D. 除非……否则

75. 他整整昏迷了一天一夜，直到昨天早晨才慢慢醒 ____。
    A. 起来　　　B. 过来
    C. 过去　　　D. 上来

76. 不要让人家 ____ 地跑了，这回还是我送去吧。
    A. 一阵一阵
    B. 一番一番
    C. 一趟一趟

D. 一下一下

77. 我曾经 _____。
    A. 住过在上海三年
    B. 三年住过在上海
    C. 在上海三年住过
    D. 在上海住过三年

78. 你在家等着，我 _____。
    A. 去吃过饭找你
    B. 吃过饭去找你
    C. 去找你吃过饭
    D. 找你去吃过饭

79. 牛肉 _____。
    A. 比猪肉要煮得时间长
    B. 要煮得时间长比猪肉
    C. 要长比猪肉煮得时间
    D. 要时间长煮得比猪肉

80. 下课铃一响，_____。
    A. 学生都跑教室出去
    B. 都跑学生教室出去
    C. 学生都跑出教室去
    D. 学生都跑出去教室

## 第5套

## 二、语法结构

（30题，20分钟）

### 第一部分

说明：51～60题，在每一个句子下面都有一个指定词语，句中 A B C D 是供选择的四个不同位置，请判断这一词语放在句子中哪个位置上恰当。

例如：

55．我们A 一起 B 去上海 C 旅游 D 过。

没有

"没有"只有放在 A 的位置上，使全句变为"我们没有一起去上海旅游过"，才合乎语法。所以第55题惟一恰当的答案是A，你应在答卷上找到号码55，在字母 A 上画一横道，横道一定要画得粗一些，重一些。

55．[A]　　[B]　　[C]　　[D]

51．他扶着 A 桌子 B 坐 C 下去 D。

慢慢

52．丁力让 A 我 B 等 C 他 D。

在这儿

53．那本小说昨天 A 我从 B 早上八点 C 看到 D 下午四点。

一直

54．我保证，A 从今以后 B 不 C 再 D 跟她来往了。

永远

55．他 A 在这里的 B 生活 C 愉快 D。

非常

56．那么 A 钱 B 一个钟头 C 数得完 D 数不完？

多

57．经过 A 紧张地 B 抢救，他终于脱离了 C 危险，我 D 松了一口气。

也

58．我们 A 班 B 同学都 C 非常喜欢听 D 孙老师讲课。

所有的

59．我 A 劝她 B 不要去，C 她 D 还是去了。

可是

60．他 A 回忆 B 起小时候 C 的生活 D。

时常

## 第二部分

说明:61~80题,每个句子中有一个或两个空儿,请在 A B C D 四个答案中选择惟一恰当的填上(在答卷上的字母上画一横道)。

例如:

67. 我昨天买了一____钢笔。

A. 件    B. 块    C. 枝    D. 条

我们只能说"我昨天买了一枝钢笔",所以第 67 题惟一恰当的答案是 C,你应在答卷上找到号码 67,在字母 C 上画一横道,横道一定要画得粗一些,重一些。

67. [A]    [B]    [C]    [D]

61. 你们学校大约有____学生?
    A. 几多    B. 多个
    C. 多少    D. 几人

62. 你们对老年妇女____称呼?
    A. 怎么    B. 什么
    C. 谁      D. 哪

63. 北京现在平均____四个高中生就有三个能上大学。
    A. 各      B. 每
    C. 分别    D. 每一

64. 刚过五点,天就开始暗____。
    A. 上来    B. 下来
    C. 出来    D. 过来

65. 你放心,这些事一天都做____完。
    A. 能      B. 会
    C. 得      D. 了

66. 我有很多话,电话里不好说,等我回到家时____当面跟你详谈。
    A. 还      B. 又
    C. 也      D. 再

67. 轰隆一声巨响,那孩子吓得____大哭。
    A. 哈哈    B. 呼呼
    C. 哇哇    D. 哗哗

68. 你到北京以后一定给家里打个电话,____爸妈惦记。
    A. 不要    B. 不叫
    C. 终止    D. 省得

69. 我____上同意你们的看法。
    A. 大概    B. 大体
    C. 大约    D. 大都

70. ____每小时 15 元计算,每月八次课共 120 元。
    A. 按      B. 就
    C. 刚      D. 也

71. 一听我的话,他的脸色____变了。
    A. 才      B. 就
    C. 刚      D. 也

72. ____酷暑严寒,他都坚持长跑,从不间断。

A. 或者  B. 也许
C. 尽管  D. 不管

73. 昨天我又买了一____床单。
    A. 片  B. 张
    C. 面  D. 条

74. 新拍的片子很多，但____看的却很少。
    A. 价值  B. 值得
    C. 能值  D. 能会

75. 我一下车，_____。
    A. 门关上就了
    B. 就门关上了
    C. 关上门就了
    D. 门就关上了

76. _____见过这本书。
    A. 我们从来没有人在图书馆里
    B. 从来没有我们人在图书馆里
    C. 在图书馆里从来没有我们人
    D. 从来在图书馆里没有人我们

77. 这几个书名_____。
    A. 你不记住记得住
    B. 你记住得记不住
    C. 你记不住记住得
    D. 你记得住记不住

78. 只有从根本上解决贫困问题，_____。
    A. 才儿童能使这里的都上学
    B. 才能使这里的儿童都能上学
    C. 才都能上学使这里的儿童
    D. 才能这里的儿童都使上学

79. 明天早上八点_____。
    A. 我们出发从学校
    B. 我们从学校出发
    C. 出发我们从学校
    D. 从学校出发我们

80. 我打算_____。
    A. 明年再中国来旅行
    B. 再来中国旅行明年
    C. 来中国旅行再明年
    D. 明年再来中国旅行

# 第6套

## 二、语法结构

（30题，20分钟）

### 第一部分

说明：51~60题，在每一个句子下面都有一个指定词语，句中 A B C D 是供选择的四个不同位置，请判断这一词语放在句子中哪个位置上恰当。

例如：

55．我们 A 一起 B 去上海 C 旅游 D 过。

没有

"没有"只有放在 A 的位置上，使全句变为"我们没有一起去上海旅游过"，才合乎语法。所以第 55 题惟一恰当的答案是 A，你应在答卷上找到号码55，在字母 A 上画一横道，横道一定要画得粗一些，重一些。

55．[A̶]　[B]　[C]　[D]

51．长江 A 比黄河 B 长 C 公里 D？

多少

52．他 A 批评 B 起 C 来，可 D 不讲情面。

人

53．A 过了整整 B 三个月，他 C 给我 D 写回信。

才

54．真是 A 做梦也 B 想不到，他 C 会做出 D 这样的事。

竟

55．考试 A 不及格，他已经够 B 难过了，你 C 别再 D 说他了。

就

56．昨天 A 我 B 到办公室 C 找了你 D，你都不在。

三趟

57．他是我 A 中学 B 时代最好 C 朋友 D。

的

58．我实在 A 不清楚 B 他究竟是 C 一个 D 人。

怎样

59．去年暑假 A 我们 B 到 C 西藏 D 了。

旅游

60．A 直到那一天，我 B 有机会 C 跟她 D 聊天。

才

## 第二部分

说明：61~80题，每个句子中有一个或两个空儿，请在 A B C D 四个答案中选择惟一恰当的填上（在答卷上的字母上画一横道）。

例如：

67. 我昨天买了一＿＿＿钢笔。
    A. 件　　B. 块　　C. 枝　　D. 条

我们只能说"我昨天买了一枝钢笔"，所以第67题惟一恰当的答案是C，你应在答卷上找到号码67，在字母C上画一横道，横道一定要画得粗一些，重一些。

67. [A]　　[B]　　[C]　　[D]

61. 上个星期天我们＿＿＿了长城。
    A. 旅游　　　　B. 旅行
    C. 游览　　　　D. 赏玩

62. 他昨天刚买了一＿＿＿台灯。
    A. 盏　　　　B. 架
    C. 座　　　　D. 个

63. 天冷＿＿＿，你要多穿点儿衣服。
    A. 着　　　　B. 过
    C. 了　　　　D. 的

64. 他打算今天下午＿＿＿＿＿＿。
    A. 还图书馆一本历史书
    B. 还一本历史书图书馆
    C. 一本历史书还图书馆
    D. 图书馆一本历史书还

65. 我＿＿＿＿＿＿，他立刻答应了。
    A. 问他去看电影
    B. 去看电影问他
    C. 请他去看电影
    D. 请去看电影他

66. 你来得真不是时候，小李＿＿＿走。
    A. 刚才　　　　B. 马上
    C. 就　　　　　D. 刚

67. 这事发生得太＿＿＿，她几乎承受不了了。
    A. 忽然　　　　B. 猛然
    C. 突然　　　　D. 骤然

68. 这个人太固执，别人的话他从来就听不＿＿＿。
    A. 进来　　　　B. 进去
    C. 上来　　　　D. 出去

69. 老师和家长＿＿＿孩子的教育问题展开了热烈讨论。
    A. 就　　　　　B. 关于
    C. 至于　　　　D. 将

70. 全院＿＿＿都在积极筹备春季运动会。
    A. 左右　　　　B. 前后
    C. 上下　　　　D. 里外

71. ＿＿＿你说什么，＿＿＿改变不了我的决心。

A. 虽然……但是
B. 即使……也
C. 既然……就
D. 无论……都

72. _____ 她真的做了对不起我的事，我_____仍然爱他。
A. 因为……所以
B. 既然……就
C. 无论……都
D. 即使……也

73. 他经常帮助我，我要_____。
A. 给他一个感谢
B. 一次感谢他
C. 给一个感谢他
D. 感谢他一次

74. 他慢慢地_____。
A. 走着在操场上
B. 在操场上走着
C. 走了在操场上
D. 走过在操场上

75. 请你_____。
A. 等我在9号楼门前5点钟
B. 等我5点钟在9号楼门前
C. 在9号楼门前等我5点钟
D. 5点钟在9号楼门前等我

76. 那个小男孩手里拿着_____。
A. 红的大大一个苹果
B. 一个红的大大苹果
C. 大大一个苹果红的
D. 一个大大的红苹果

77. 无论什么时候，他都_____。
A. 给很多帮助我
B. 给我很多帮助
C. 很多给我帮助
D. 给帮助我很多

78. 他们经常没钱，但是_____。
A. 不轻易问朋友帮助
B. 问朋友借钱不轻易
C. 不轻易求朋友帮助
D. 求朋友帮助不轻易

79. 如果接不到你的信，_____。
A. 就我不去你那儿了
B. 就我不来你那儿了
C. 我就你那儿不来了
D. 我就不去你那儿了

80. 我在那儿等你，希望_____。
A. 你很快来看我
B. 你来看我很快
C. 你去看我很快
D. 你很快去看我

# 第7套

## 二、语法结构

（30题，20分钟）

### 第一部分

说明：51～60题，在每一个句子下面都有一个指定词语，句中ＡＢＣＤ是供选择的四个不同位置，请判断这一词语放在句子中哪个位置上恰当。

例如：

　　55．我们A 一起 B 去上海 C 旅游 D 过。

　　　　　没有

"没有"只有放在A的位置上，使全句变为"我们没有一起去上海旅游过"，才合乎语法。所以第55题惟一恰当的答案是A，你应在答卷上找到号码55，在字母A上画一横道，横道一定要画得粗一些，重一些。

　　55．[★]　[B]　[C]　[D]

51．A 你的身体 B 不舒服，C 他 D 应该照顾你。
　　　　　　就

52．她决定 A 参加 B 足球 C 比赛 D。
　　　　　　　　　　了

53．要 A 想学习 B 成绩好，C 就 D 下苦功夫。
　　　　　　　必须

54．A 没有 B 比写匿名信告黑状 C 卑鄙 D 恶毒的事了。
　　　　　　　　更

55．请代 A 我问 B 你的 C 父母 D。
　　　　　　　好

56．A 我 B 喜欢 C 他写的散文 D，还喜欢他写的小说。
　　不仅

57．他查阅了杂志，A 却 B 没有找到 C 他 D 需要的那篇文章。
　　　　　　然而

58．A 不要 B 吃和穿 C 上花 D 太多时间。
　　　　　　　　在

59．你 A 看得出 B 看 C 出这封信是 D 谁写的？
　　　　　　　　不

60．老师 A 班长通知 B 大家 C 明天早上5点钟 D 在校门口集合上车。
　　让

## 第二部分

说明:61~80题,每个句子中有一个或两个空儿,请在 A B C D 四个答案中选择惟一恰当的填上(在答卷上的字母上画一横道)。

例如:
67. 我昨天买了一____钢笔。
  A. 件    B. 块    C. 枝    D. 条

我们只能说"我昨天买了一枝钢笔",所以第67题惟一恰当的答案是C,你应在答卷上找到号码67,在字母C上画一横道,横道一定要画得粗一些,重一些。

67. [A]    [B]    [C]    [D]

---

61. 人____要死的,这是无法抗拒的自然规律。
  A. 终于         B. 总是
  C. 根本         D. 始终

62. 他还没明白怎么回事,____被打了一耳光。
  A. 才           B. 刚
  C. 就           D. 再

63. 人家的孩子能上大学,____我们的孩子就不能上吗?
  A. 为什么       B. 何况
  C. 难怪         D. 难道

64. 她____数学,也精通天文、地理和化学。
  A. 善于         B. 擅长
  C. 特长         D. 拿手

65. 你太客气了,____弄得大家很拘束。
  A. 偏偏         B. 反正
  C. 反而         D. 并且

66. 我到这来已经两个月了,生活上还不习惯,我很____我的爸爸妈妈。
  A. 想想         B. 想
  C. 想一想       D. 想了想

67. 这____电视剧的女主角是我的中学同学。
  A. 本           B. 片
  C. 位           D. 部

68. 这个礼堂只有八百个席位,估计全校师生都来肯定坐不____。
  A. 下           B. 进
  C. 里           D. 住

69. 经过三个月的治疗,她恢复了健康,____开始工作了。
  A. 重           B. 再
  C. 又           D. 复

70. 听了女儿的话,母亲_____。
  A. 半天考虑了才下决心
  B. 才考虑了半天下决心
  C. 考虑了才半天下决心
  D. 考虑了半天才下决心

模拟练习·第7套    121

71. ____ 把全校学生发动起来，____ 单靠我们俩是救不了他的。
    A. 只要……就
    B. 只有……才
    C. 固然……也
    D. 除非……否则

72. 孩子太小，学 ____ 这么多课程。
    A. 不了    B. 不及
    C. 不得    D. 不行

73. 我听说她 _____ 。
    A. 已经毕业大学了
    B. 已经大学毕业了
    C. 毕业大学已经了
    D. 大学毕业已经了

74. 昨天 _____ 。
    A. 我见面我朋友了
    B. 我再见我朋友了
    C. 我视我朋友了
    D. 我见到我朋友了

75. 我经常看见他俩 _____ 。
    A. 一起看在电影
    B. 在一起看电影
    C. 电影在看一起
    D. 在看电影一起

76. 今天我感觉浑身没劲，还 _____ 。
    A. 一点肚子疼
    B. 肚子疼上点
    C. 肚子疼有点
    D. 有点肚子疼

77. 我相信不久的将来你 _____ 。
    A. 汉语会说得很好
    B. 会汉语说得很好
    C. 很好会说得汉语
    D. 很好汉语会说得

78. 请你 _____ ，可以吗？
    A. 借我把你的词典用用
    B. 借我用用把你的词典
    C. 把你的词典借我用用
    D. 用用把你的词典借我

79. 她那种 _____ ，真令人作呕。
    A. 神气劲儿把谁都不放在眼里的
    B. 神气劲儿谁都不把放在眼里的
    C. 谁都把放不在眼里的神气劲儿
    D. 把谁都不放在眼里的神气劲儿

80. 我们 _____ 。
    A. 可以玩几天痛痛快快地
    B. 玩几天可以痛痛快快地
    C. 可以痛痛快快地玩几天
    D. 痛痛快快地可以玩几天

# 第8套

## 二、语法结构
（30题，20分钟）

### 第一部分

说明：51～60题，在每一个句子下面都有一个指定词语，句中 A B C D 是供选择的四个不同位置，请判断这一词语放在句子中哪个位置上恰当。

例如：

    55. 我们 A 一起 B 去上海 C 旅游 D 过。

            没有

"没有"只有放在 A 的位置上，使全句变为"我们没有一起去上海旅游过"，才合乎语法。所以第 55 题惟一恰当的答案是 A，你应在答卷上找到号码 55，在字母 A 上画一横道，横道一定要画得粗一些，重一些。

    55. [★]   [B]   [C]   [D]

51. 我非常 A 想说 B 汉语，但是 C 我只 D 说一点儿。

                    会

52. A 他的成绩 B 在我们班里 C 还算是 D 好的。

                    比较

53. 学校 A 同意 B 他 C 从长期班 D 转入短期班吗？

                    能

54. 大家都 A 说他 B 弹钢琴 C 弹 D 特别好。

                    得

55. 他 A 去 B 图书馆 C 借一本书 D。

                  要

56. A 以后 B 我们 C 要生产 D 更多的机器。

                  一定

57. 我一直 A 以为 B 我是你所 C 爱的 D 人。

                  惟一

58. 你 A 就不理他，B 看他 C 把你 D 怎么样。

                  敢

59. 他 A 再三 B 声明自己 C 是清白的，但 D 没有人相信他。

                  却

60. A 跟这样 B 一个 C 不知耻的人，还有 D 可说的。

                  什么

## 第二部分

说明:61~80题,每个句子中有一个或两个空儿,请在ＡＢＣＤ四个答案中选择惟一恰当的填上(在答卷上的字母上画一横道)。

例如:

67. 我昨天买了一____钢笔。

A. 件    B. 块    C. 枝    D. 条

我们只能说"我昨天买了一枝钢笔",所以第67题惟一恰当的答案是C,你应在答卷上找到号码67,在字母C上画一横道,横道一定要画得粗一些,重一些。

67. [★]    [B]    [C]    [D]

61. 直到这两天我____发现,他身上也有许多优点。
 A. 再          B. 就
 C. 却          D. 才

62. 李永强是五年前参加工作的,____他只有18岁。
 A. 此时        B. 当时
 C. 过时        D. 历时

63. 新事物不断涌现,旧事物不断消亡,这是社会发展的____趋势。
 A. 必然        B. 必要
 C. 必定        D. 必须

64. 这次出国的机会十分难得,你可____别错过。
 A. 万一        B. 千万
 C. 一万        D. 万分

65. 我今年17岁,____过一年就18了。
 A. 又          B. 第二
 C. 再          D. 下一个

66. 他出了车祸,但____医生们全力抢救,现在已经脱离了危险。
 A. 经历        B. 经常
 C. 经过        D. 度过

67. 舒适、美观的休闲服装在市场____越来越受欢迎。
 A. 上          B. 里
 C. 中间        D. 下

68. 我一个人怎么吃得____这么多东西。
 A. 下          B. 上
 C. 没了        D. 完成

69. 她这个人就这样,不管遇到什么事,____唠唠叨叨没完没了。
 A. 总之        B. 总是
 C. 总算        D. 还是

70. ____天气如何,运动会____照常举行。
 A. 虽然……但
 B. 既然……就

C. 即使……也
D. 无论……都

71. 一看见他那 ____ 得意洋洋的样子，我就恶心。
    A. 张　　　　B. 派
    C. 份　　　　D. 副

72. 整整20年没见，他的头发已经花白，我 ____ 认不出他了。
    A. 终于　　　B. 简直
    C. 毕竟　　　D. 总算

73. 春节 ____ 那个城市连续发生了三起火灾。
    A. 左右　　　B. 上下
    C. 先后　　　D. 前后

74. 昨天你那个朋友说话 ____ 不客气。
    A. 怎么那么
    B. 怎么多么
    C. 怎么果然
    D. 怎么明明

75. 他们班的女孩子 ____ 爱打扮。
    A. 一个像一个
    B. 一个跟一个
    C. 一个同一个
    D. 一个比一个

76. 你来 ____ ，他来 ____ ，只要是为这事，我都不欢迎。
    A. 也行……也行
    B. 也能……也能
    C. 也好……也好
    D. 也要也要

77. 我知道你 _____ 。
    A. 把这件衣服能洗干净
    B. 能洗干净把这件衣服
    C. 这件衣服能把洗干净
    D. 能把这件衣服洗干净

78. 下飞机后，我们 _____ 就到那儿了。
    A. 再坐了汽车一个小时
    B. 又坐了一个小时汽车
    C. 又坐了汽车一个小时
    D. 再坐了一个小时汽车

79. 你 _____ 给我们介绍一下。
    A. 把你的学习方法能不能
    B. 能把你的学习方法不能
    C. 把能不能你的学习方法
    D. 能不能把你的学习方法

80. 我到北京以后 _____ ，请原谅。
    A. 没有立刻给你写信
    B. 立刻没有给你写信
    C. 没有写信立刻给你
    D. 立刻没有写信给你

## 第9套

### 二、语法结构

（30题，20分钟）

### 第一部分

说明：51~60题，在每一个句子下面都有一个指定词语，句中ABCD是供选择的四个不同位置，请判断这一词语放在句子中哪个位置上恰当。
例如：

    55．我们A一起B去上海C旅游D过。
        没有

"没有"只有放在A的位置上，使全句变为"我们没有一起去上海旅游过"，才合乎语法。所以第55题惟一恰当的答案是A，你应在答卷上找到号码55，在字母A上画一横道，横道一定要画得粗一些，重一些。

    55．[★]  [B]  [C]  [D]

51．A是周末，他们相聚在B李明家，说说C笑笑，D真是热闹。
    又

52．像他A那样的B大好人，世上C有D几个呢？
    能

53．A他们B举办多次C校外活动，还D没出过事故。
    从来

54．他A在公共汽车上B偷钱包C大家抓住D送往公安局了。
    被

55．A现在B他C在操场上D打排球。
    正

56．已经A深夜了，他B在灯下认认C真真地D看书。
    还

57．A我B把这本小说C翻译D成中文。
    能

58．A他的女儿B该上C中学了D。
    已经

59．今天A再忙，我B要C把这个材料D看完。
    也

60．没有A一个人B想起这位C无私的捕鼠者D。
    再

## 第二部分

说明：61～80题，每个句子中有一个或两个空儿，请在 Ａ Ｂ Ｃ Ｄ 四个答案中选择惟一恰当的填上（在答卷上的字母上画一横道）。

例如：

　　67．我昨天买了一____钢笔。

　　　　Ａ．件　　Ｂ．块　　Ｃ．枝　　Ｄ．条

我们只能说"我昨天买了一枝钢笔"，所以第 67 题惟一恰当的答案是 C，你应在答卷上找到号码 67，在字母 C 上画一横道，横道一定要画得粗一些，重一些。

　　67．[A]　　[B]　　[C̶]　　[D]

61．今天天气很暖和____到山里去玩儿。
　　A．合适　　　　B．适合
　　C．方便　　　　D．适值

62．他的发言清楚____流利。
　　A．和　　　　　B．跟
　　C．又　　　　　D．再

63．外面这么冷，你快进屋吧，别____了凉。
　　A．得　　　　　B．着
　　C．冻　　　　　D．病

64．做菜时少放点盐，他气管不好，____咸一点就咳嗽个没完。
　　A．很少　　　　B．微小
　　C．只有　　　　D．稍微

65．她今天打扮得可真____的。
　　A．漂亮　　　　B．挺漂亮
　　C．漂里漂亮　　D．漂漂亮亮

66．5 年不见，爸爸可比以前____多了。
　　A．旧　　　　　B．年长
　　C．年岁　　　　D．老

67．我____学弹钢琴，但没有老师教。
　　A．想想　　　　B．想一想
　　C．想　　　　　D．想了想

68．她突然觉得自己的丈夫很____。
　　A．私人　　　　B．自私
　　C．私自　　　　D．隐私

69．____我不是她的亲生女儿，____她待我却像亲妈一样。
　　A．既然……就
　　B．因为……所以
　　C．只要……就
　　D．虽然……但

70．快叫他们到这里____。
　　A．避雨一遍
　　B．避一下雨
　　C．避一遍雨
　　D．避雨一下

71. 我的汉语 _____ 。
   A. 说得不好
   B. 说好不得
   C. 不说得好
   D. 不好说得

72. 昨天晚上 11 点 _____ 。
   A. 才我回到宿舍
   B. 我才回到宿舍
   C. 我回到才宿舍
   D. 才宿舍我回到

73. ____ 你已经不顾兄弟情分，也 ____ 别怪我不客气了。
   A. 因为……所以
   B. 即使……就
   C. 既然……就
   D. 虽然……但是

74. 这里秋天不常刮风，但经常 _____ 。
   A. 不下雨   B. 下小雨
   C. 小雨下   D. 下雨小

75. 这台机器整整修了 ____ 。
   A. 两来天   B. 两多天
   C. 两天多   D. 多两天

76. 这所大学有 _____ 。
   A. 两千个人左右
   B. 两千左右个人
   C. 左右两千个人
   D. 个人两千左右

77. 我保证这件衣服 _____ 。
   A. 没有再便宜不过的了
   B. 没有不过再便宜的了
   C. 不过没有便宜的了
   D. 再便宜不过了

78. _____ 一下吗？
   A. 可以你的词典借用
   B. 你的词典借用可以
   C. 借用你的词典可以
   D. 你的词典可以借用

79. 这封信寄到 _____ 。
   A. 学院路 15 号北京市海淀区
   B. 15 号学院路海淀区北京市
   C. 北京市学院路海淀区 15 号
   D. 北京市海淀区学院路 15 号

80. 他身高一米七，只 _____ 。
   A. 比我高一点儿
   B. 比我一点儿高
   C. 一点儿高比我
   D. 高一点儿比我

# 第10套

## 二、语法结构

（30题，20分钟）

### 第一部分

说明：51～60题，在每一个句子下面都有一个指定词语，句中 A B C D 是供选择的四个不同位置，请判断这一词语放在句子中哪个位置上恰当。

例如：

　　55．我们 A 一起 B 去上海 C 旅游 D 过。

　　　　　没有

"没有"只有放在 A 的位置上，使全句变为"我们没有一起去上海旅游过"，才合乎语法。所以第55题惟一恰当的答案是 A，你应在答卷上找到号码55，在字母 A 上画一横道，横道一定要画得粗一些，重一些。

　　55．[★]　[B]　[C]　[D]

51．A 一定 B 向你弟弟 C 道歉 D。
　　　　　替我

52．刚才 A 他又 B 说 C 了一顿 D。
　　　　　　被总编

53．A 老师 B 没走，学生们 C 就开始 D 打闹起来。
　　　　　　　　　还

54．他 A 在北海住 B 了一个 C 月 D。
　　　　　　　　多

55．全班 A 除了李华外，谁 B 不知道他 C 住哪儿 D。
　　　　　　　　也

56．天气很冷，A 快 B 进 C 屋里 D 吧。
　　　　　　　去

57．A 三年前我就 B 去 C 德国 D。
　　　　　　　　　过

58．现在 A 请你 B 自我 C 介绍一下 D 吧。
　　　　　　　　　给我们

59．她 A 长得 B 没有 C 小张 D 漂亮。
　　　　　　　　那么

60．刚才 A 我看见小李 B 跑 C 下山去 D。
　　　　　　　　　　了

## 第二部分

说明：61～80题，每个句子中有一个或两个空儿，请在 A B C D 四个答案中选择惟一恰当的填上（在答卷上的字母上画一横道）。

例如：

　　67．我昨天买了一____钢笔。

　　　A．件　　B．块　　C．枝　　D．条

我们只能说"我昨天买了一枝钢笔"，所以第 67 题惟一恰当的答案是 C，你应在答卷上找到号码 67，在字母 C 上画一横道，横道一定要画得粗一些，重一些。

　　67．[A]　　[B]　　[C]　　[D]

61．你千万____拒绝我的邀请。
　A．没　　　　　B．不
　C．别　　　　　D．没有

62．周荣是个好学生，大家都该____她学习。
　A．对　　　　　B．向
　C．把　　　　　D．关于

63．在一定的条件____，事物会向相反方向转化。
　A．上　　　　　B．里
　C．下　　　　　D．内

64．亏你____是个领导呢，一点道理都不讲。
　A．还　　　　　B．才
　C．却　　　　　D．只

65．从他的家____马老师的家很近。
　A．离　　　　　B．离开
　C．到　　　　　D．距离

66．最近我和他都比较____。
　A．挺忙的　　　B．很忙

　C．忙　　　　　D．忙极了

67．____天气预报，明天有大雨。
　A．根据　　　　B．按照
　C．由于　　　　D．依照

68．我____要打电话找你，你来了。
　A．正　　　　　B．在
　C．当　　　　　D．及时

69．北京的冬天常常____。
　A．刮大风　　　B．大刮风
　C．很刮风　　　D．很刮大风

70．商场里的人_____？
　A．多极了不多极了
　B．多极不极了
　C．极多不极多
　D．多不多

71．我和我的朋友们都_____。
　A．喜欢这个学校了
　B．喜欢了这个学校
　C．把这个学校喜欢了
　D．喜欢了把这个学校

72. 王刚 _____ 走进宿舍了。
    A. 拿了东西很多
    B. 拿着东西很多
    C. 拿着很多东西
    D. 拿得很多东西

73. 他去 _____ 吃饭。
    A. 离学校比较远的地方
    B. 学校比较远离的地方
    C. 比较远的地方离学校
    D. 比较学校远离的地方

74. 她脱下大衣,把它 _____ 。
    A. 挂着在墙上
    B. 挂了在墙上
    C. 挂在墙上了
    D. 挂在着墙上

75. 借我 _____ ,好吗?
    A. 看一下杂志你借来的
    B. 看杂志一下你借来的
    C. 看你借来的杂志一下
    D. 看一下你借来的杂志

76. 他们 _____ 。
    A. 很便宜买东西的
    B. 买东西的很便宜
    C. 买的东西很便宜
    D. 便宜的很买东西

77. 他强迫女儿 _____ 。
    A. 住在一起跟一个有钱人
    B. 在一起住跟一个有钱人
    C. 跟一个有钱人住在一起
    D. 住在跟一个有钱人一起

78. 我还没有看完 _____ 呢!
    A. 你给介绍那本小说
    B. 你介绍那本小说给我
    C. 你那本小说介绍给我
    D. 你介绍给我的那本小说

79. _____ 五十分钟。
    A. 昨天的开会进行了
    B. 进行了开会昨天
    C. 开会进行了昨天
    D. 昨天的会进行了

80. 那辆自行车 _____ 。
    A. 让人没骑走
    B. 没让人走骑
    C. 没让人骑走
    D. 让人骑没走

# 中国汉语水平考试语法结构
## （初、中等）模拟练习答案

**第1套**

51. C  52. C  53. C  54. A  55. B
56. C  57. C  58. C  59. B  60. C
61. D  62. B  63. A  64. C  65. B
66. D  67. B  68. B  69. C  70. B
71. A  72. B  73. D  74. A  75. D
76. A  77. D  78. C  79. B  80. D

**第2套**

51. A  52. B  53. A  54. B  55. C
56. C  57. B  58. C  59. B  60. B
61. B  62. A  63. B  64. D  65. C
66. B  67. A  68. B  69. D  70. B
71. C  72. A  73. C  74. B  75. A
76. B  77. A  78. D  79. A  80. D

**第3套**

51. C  52. B  53. D  54. C  55. C
56. C  57. B  58. B  59. B  60. A
61. D  62. B  63. C  64. A  65. B
66. A  67. D  68. B  69. D  70. A
71. D  72. C  73. D  74. D  75. C
76. B  77. D  78. A  79. C  80. B

**第4套**

51. A  52. B  53. C  54. A  55. D
56. A  57. C  58. A  59. C  60. C
61. B  62. D  63. A  64. C  65. D
66. D  67. C  68. B  69. C  70. D

71. B　72. C　73. D　74. D　75. B
76. C　77. D　78. B　79. A　80. C

## 第5套

51. B　52. B　53. C　54. B　55. C
56. A　57. D　58. B　59. C　60. A
61. C　62. A　63. B　64. B　65. C
66. D　67. C　68. D　69. B　70. A
71. B　72. D　73. D　74. B　75. D
76. A　77. D　78. B　79. B　80. D

## 第6套

51. C　52. C　53. C　54. C　55. C
56. D　57. C　58. C　59. D　60. B
61. C　62. A　63. C　64. A　65. C
66. D　67. C　68. B　69. A　70. C
71. D　72. D　73. D　74. B　75. D
76. D　77. B　78. C　79. D　80. D

## 第7套

51. D　52. D　53. D　54. C　55. D
56. B　57. A　58. B　59. C　60. A
61. B　62. C　63. D　64. B　65. C
66. B　67. D　68. A　69. C　70. D
71. D　72. A　73. B　74. D　75. B
76. D　77. A　78. C　79. D　80. C

## 第8套

51. D　52. D　53. A　54. D　55. A
56. C　57. C　58. C　59. D　60. D
61. D　62. B　63. A　64. B　65. C
66. C　67. A　68. A　69. B　70. D
71. D　72. B　73. D　74. A　75. D
76. C　77. D　78. B　79. D　80. A

**第 9 套**

| 51. A | 52. C | 53. D | 54. C | 55. C |
| 56. B | 57. B | 58. B | 59. B | 60. B |
| 61. B | 62. C | 63. B | 64. D | 65. B |
| 66. D | 67. C | 68. B | 69. D | 70. B |
| 71. A | 72. B | 73. C | 74. B | 75. C |
| 76. A | 77. D | 78. D | 79. D | 80. A |

**第 10 套**

| 51. B | 52. B | 53. B | 54. C | 55. B |
| 56. D | 57. C | 58. B | 59. D | 60. D |
| 61. C | 62. B | 63. C | 64. A | 65. C |
| 66. C | 67. A | 68. A | 69. A | 70. D |
| 71. A | 72. C | 73. A | 74. C | 75. D |
| 76. C | 77. C | 78. D | 79. D | 80. C |